£0   £1.49

v.k £6

Thomas Cook **pocket** guides

MADRID

Thomas
Cook

Written by Nick Inman and Clara Villanueva
Updated by Clara Villanueva

Published by Thomas Cook Publishing
A division of Thomas Cook Tour Operations Limited
Company registration no. 3772199 England
The Thomas Cook Business Park, 9 Coningsby Road,
Peterborough PE3 8SB, United Kingdom
Email: books@thomascook.com, Tel: +44 (0) 1733 416477
www.thomascookpublishing.com

Produced by Cambridge Publishing Management Limited
Burr Elm Court, Main Street, Caldecote CB23 7NU
www.cambridgepm.co.uk

ISBN: 978-1-84848-335-4

© 2006, 2008 Thomas Cook Publishing
This third edition © 2010
Text © Thomas Cook Publishing
Maps © Thomas Cook Publishing/PCGraphics (UK) Limited
Transport map © Communicarta Limited

Series Editor: Karen Beaulah
Production/DTP: Steven Collins

Printed and bound in Spain by GraphyCems

Cover photography © Stock Connection Blue/Alamy

CONTENTS

SYMBOLS KEY

The following symbols are used throughout this book:

ⓐ address ⓣ telephone ⓦ website address ⓔ email
ⓞ opening times ⓝ public transport connections ⓘ important

The following symbols are used on the maps:

𝑖	information office	▦	points of interest
✈	airport	◯	city
➕	hospital	O	large town
⊘	police station	○	small town
🚌	bus station	▬	motorway
🚆	railway station	—	main road
Ⓜ	metro	—	minor road
✝	cathedral	—	railway
❶	numbers denote featured cafés & restaurants		

Hotels and restaurants are graded by approximate price as follows:
£ budget price ££ mid-range price £££ expensive

▶ *Statue of King Philip III in the Plaza Mayor*

INTRODUCING
Madrid

Introduction

From inauspicious beginnings as a landlocked hamlet next to an insignificant trickle of a river, in the last 500 years Madrid has grown to become one of the great capitals of Europe, attracting millions of visitors each year. Between eating delicious tapas, seeing Velázquez masterpieces, partying till dawn in the nightclubs and visiting the impossibly opulent palaces and gardens, the only danger is to try to see – and eat – too much. In anything less than a very long weekend, you'll find it hard to fit in everything Madrid and its surroundings have to offer unless you rush around at breakneck speed. Which would be to miss the point of life in Spain – where the cardinal rule is to pace yourself and make the most of each moment.

If you have the stamina, you could easily spend an entire weekend exploring three of the world's greatest art galleries, barely stepping outside into the sunshine between them. And that's without tackling the city's many curious, lesser-known museums.

In complete contrast, the city's other attraction is its sociability. This is a city that works hard but plays harder. Whether your taste is for mooching about in arty cafés, tapas-bar hopping, raving the night away in pumped-up clubs or enjoying romantic gourmet dining in posh restaurants, Madrid won't disappoint.

You'll find the city centre compact enough to get around quickly and easily, often on foot. On the way you'll discover atmospheric medieval streets, grand boulevards lined with a variety of shops from the tiny and quaint to the garish and trendy, monumental squares and delightful gardens.

If the length of your stay allows, you'll probably want to turn the city's location to your advantage and make it a base for exploring central Spain. The famous palace-monastery of El Escorial is within easy reach, as are the great cities of Toledo, Salamanca, Segovia and Ávila – each permeated with history and crammed with sights.

● *The beautiful painted façade of the Casa de la Panadería*

When to go

The best time to visit Madrid is in either spring or autumn, when it is warm enough to enjoy the café terraces and parks but cool enough to stroll about at midday; these are also the seasons when local festivities are most abundant. Anyone hardy enough to visit in the scorching summer months will have to copy the locals and take a siesta; this is also the season when tour buses unload on Madrid and there can be long queues for the main attractions.

SEASONS & CLIMATE

Being high up on the Castilian *meseta*, the plateau of central Spain, and far from cooling coastal influences, Madrid endures very cold winters and very hot summers. The locals famously describe it as '*nueve meses de invierno, tres meses de infierno*' (nine months of winter, three months of hell). Spring and autumn are short seasons but are the best times to visit. The city is at its most peaceful in winter, which can be bitingly cold. The streets are quieter as high summer sets in, too, but for a

● *Religious procession during Semana Santa*

different reason: rising temperatures mean that many *madrileños* only come out of their air-conditioned offices and homes at night. August is holiday time and many Spaniards decamp to the coast or the countryside leaving some businesses and sights closed until September. Whenever you visit, be ready for sudden changes of temperature. It's a good idea at any time of year to pack a hat and some suncream.

ANNUAL EVENTS

ⓘ Exact dates of events may change from year to year – so check
ⓦ www.munimadrid.es

January–February

Cabalgata de Reyes (night of 5 Jan). Although Father Christmas is increasingly popular, most Spanish children still get their presents from the Three Kings at Epiphany (6 Jan). The evening before, Twelfth Night, there is a colourful procession of decorated floats from the Parque del Retiro, along Calle de Alcalá, to the Plaza Mayor, with the three kings handing out sweets and crowns to the crowds of children lining the route.

Carnaval (Carnival; between early Feb and early Mar). Madrid celebrates the run-up to Lent with fancy-dress parties and a parade from Plaza de Colón to Plaza de Cibeles, ending in a comic parade on Shrove Tuesday called the *Entierro de la Sardina* (Burial of the Sardine) from the Old Town to the Casa de Campo.

March–April

Semana Santa (Easter Week; Mar or Apr). Processions of spookily hooded penitents bearing images of Christ and the Virgin take place before Easter. The best place to see the floats is La Latina quarter on Maundy Thursday and Good Friday.

Día de Cervantes (23 Apr; Cervantes' Day & World Book Day). Book fair in the outlying town of Alcalá de Henares, birthplace of the author of *Don Quixote*.

May

Dos de Mayo (2 May). Madrid commemorates a rebellion against French occupying forces in 1808 with festivities, including free music concerts in the Plaza Dos de Mayo and the Parque Las Vistillas in the Malasaña district.

Fiesta de San Isidro (15 May). The city celebrates its patron saint with traditional ceremonies and a roster of other events (see pages 12–13).

Corpus Christi (between mid-May and mid-June). An occasion for religious processions; the most spectacular are in nearby Toledo.

Feria del Libro (last week of May). Prestigious book fair in the Parque del Retiro with plenty of signings by well-known authors.

June–July

San Antonio de la Florida (13 June). Single women in search of a husband attend a traditional ceremony in the Ermita de San Antonio de la Florida. Events are held in the adjacent Parque de la Bombilla.

Los Veranos de la Villa (July–mid-Sept). Madrid stages a series of concerts, often featuring internationally famous artists and entertainment.

August–September

Verbenas de San Cayetano, San Lorenzo & La Paloma Street parties are organised in the neighbourhoods of Lavapiés, Rastro and La Latina. Expect a family atmosphere with traditional dress, chotis dancing (a style that's typical of Madrid) and sangria-sodden barbecues.

Festival de Otoño (mid-Sept–mid-Oct). Drama festival in various venues around the city.

November

Todos los Santos (1 Nov; All Saints' Day). People remember their departed loved ones by decorating cemeteries with flowers. Bakeries sell a special sweet for the occasion, *huesos de santo*, literally 'saints' bones'.

Romería de San Eugenio (14 Nov). Men and women in *castizo* (or traditional) costumes drive in open carriages to El Monte del Pardo to have a picnic, and to sing and dance.

December

Noche Vieja (31 Dec). The Puerta del Sol is crammed with revellers to welcome in the New Year and the nation watches on TV. The tradition is to eat 12 grapes to the beat of the chimes of midnight and then drink *cava*, the Spanish equivalent of champagne. Don't forget your lucky red underwear!

PUBLIC HOLIDAYS

Año Nuevo (New Year's Day) 1 Jan
Día de Reyes (Epiphany) 6 Jan
Jueves Santo (Maundy Thursday) Mar or Apr
Viernes Santo (Good Friday) Mar or Apr
Día del Trabajo (Labour Day) 1 May
La Asunción (Assumption) 15 Aug
Día de la Hispanidad (Spain's National Day) 12 Oct
Todos Los Santos (All Saints' Day) 1 Nov
Día de la Constitución (Constitution Day) 6 Dec
La Inmaculada Concepción (Immaculate Conception) 8 Dec
Día de Navidad (Christmas Day) 25 Dec

Fiesta de San Isidro

May in Madrid seems like one long month of festivities. First comes Dos de Mayo (2 May), when the city commemorates an uprising against the French occupying forces in 1808. Scarcely a week later celebrations begin again ostensibly in honour of the city's patron saint, San Isidro Labrador (St Isidore), a 12th-century farm labourer. His feast day is 15 May and, while there is still a core of traditional ceremony, everything ancient and pious is swamped by the modern fiesta with its craft markets, rock concerts and art exhibitions going on non-stop for ten days in the middle of the month.

A major and essential component is the Feria Taurina de San Isidro, an extended run of bullfights that spills over into June. It is considered to be the most prestigious bullfighting event in the world and draws top matadors and celebrity spectators.

On the morning of 15 May itself, there is a colourful *romería* (pilgrimage en masse) to the shrine of the saint, the Ermita de San Isidro, across the Río Manzanares from the Puerta de Toledo, a scene that once inspired Goya. In the evening a procession of religious floats, devotees of the saint and ecclesiastical and civil dignitaries leaves the Iglesia de San Isidro to do the rounds of the Old Town. It is followed by concerts and dancing in the Plaza Mayor and the Jardines de las Vistillas, and a firework display.

Much in evidence all the while are the *castizos*, the people who claim to be the authentic *madrileños*, wearing traditional dress – women in long, spotted dresses, headscarf and shawl, and men in checked or dark trousers, black jacket, flat cap and neck choker.

If you're in Madrid in May, and the religious rites, *castizo* displays and the bulls are not to your fancy, you can still have a good time. For most people – city residents and visitors alike – the Fiesta de San

Isidro is one big excuse for going out and partying, in a month that usually brings Madrid some good weather.

⬤ *All the fun of the fair at the Fiesta de San Isidro*

History

Madrid started out in the ninth century as Magerit, an obscure Moorish garrison defending the frontier between the Islamic kingdom of Al-Andalus in the south and the Catholic kingdoms to the north. After the Moors were defeated, it became an inconsequential backwater, barely even marked on the map. Madrid became the capital of Spain only in 1561, when King Felipe II transferred the imperial court from nearby Toledo.

From then on, the fabulous quantities of gold arriving from the colonies of the New World were used to build a city fit for a court and aristocracy to live in. Palaces, mansions, avenues, squares and gardens were laid out as the city entered its 'Golden Age', represented by the paintings of Velázquez and El Greco, the plays of Lope de Vega and that masterpiece of Spanish literature, *Don Quixote* by Miguel de Cervantes.

The accession to the throne by the first of the Bourbon monarchs in 1701 sparked a fresh wave of building over the next century, this time with an unmistakably French influence.

But early in the next century, disaster struck when Spain was occupied by the troops of Napoleon. On 2 May 1808 the population of Madrid rebelled against the French occupier. The following day Spanish patriots were rounded up and executed by firing squad, an event indelibly marked in the city's memory and the subject of a famous painting by Goya.

The 19th and early 20th centuries were turbulent times for Spain and its capital. Leaders, regimes and constitutions came and went, with Madrid the battleground for all political upheavals. Things reached a head in July 1936, when General Francisco Franco rebelled against the elected government of the day, unleashing the fratricidal bloodshed of the Spanish Civil War. One of his first acts was to besiege Madrid, but the city held out for the Republic for three years before being forced to capitulate.

The war over, an exhausted Madrid became the capital of a repressive dictatorship that lasted almost 40 years. Many people expected Franco's death in 1975 to spark a return to political instability but instead Spain was converted into a constitutional monarchy in which King Juan Carlos I presides over an elected government based in Madrid.

During the 1980s Madrid became renowned for La Movida Madrileña, an uninhibited time of personal and cultural freedom. The defeat of a right-wing coup d'etat in 1981 proved that Spain had finally turned its back on authoritarian government. Poignantly, in the same year Picasso's anti-war painting *Guernica* – which the artist ordered to be brought back to Spain only when democracy was secured – arrived in Madrid and now hangs in the Centro de Arte Reina Sofía.

As the capital city, Madrid is often the venue for public mass demonstrations. In 2003 over a million people marched in protest against Spanish involvement in the Iraq invasion. This was followed by widespread anger after the horrific terrorist attack on the city's rail network on 11 March 2004, which killed 191 people, and the ETA car bomb that destroyed a car park at Barajas airport in 2006. Spain, and with it Madrid, has been hit hard by the recession, not least because it had staked much of its economic hopes on a building boom that had been going on for two decades. This created jobs and inflated property prices but has left in its wake unemployment and hence less cash in circulation. However, it is not for nothing that *madrileños* are nicknamed *gatos* (cats) – a walk down the crowded noisy streets at 4am on a Saturday night confirms that the party is nowhere near over yet.

Lifestyle

When do *madrileños* sleep – or get any work done, come to that – if they always seem to be out living the good life? It's a question often asked by visitors and the answer is that the citizens know how to combine work and play, and how to pace themselves. You'll get the most out of your stay if you adjust yourself to the city's rhythm.

Most *madrileños* get up as early for work as everyone else in Europe, even after a night out, but they will not have breakfast (often in a bar) until around 10.00. They know they have to keep going until Spain's late lunchtime at 14.00 or 15.00. This is followed by a long digestive break, and many shops, offices and tourist sights do not open again until 17.00 (considered the beginning of the afternoon). Many people still have half a working day left before clocking off at 20.00 or even 21.00, and having dinner at 22.00 or even 23.00. Then they are ready to go out late and stay out late, and in summer the pavements can still be crowded at 04.00.

To keep up with them, there are some golden rules. Not everyone has a siesta but at least be sure to have a rest in the middle of the day. Most Spaniards drink to be sociable, not to get drunk, and they invariably eat something with a glass of wine or beer – hence the existence of tapas.

The people of Madrid are generally welcoming to visitors, even if there is a language barrier to overcome, but you will get on much better with them if you pay attention to local customs. Particularly important in this gregarious country is to show respect for other people. Always say 'hello' when you enter a shop, bar or any other public place: *buenos días* during the day and *buenas tardes* (good afternoon) from about 19.00 or 20.00.

If you eavesdrop on any conversation in Madrid, it won't take long before the topic turns to the dramatic rise in the cost of living. Real estate is now more expensive here than anywhere else in Spain but rising prices in other areas, from taxis to clothes and hotels, mean that the capital is no longer a cheap holiday option.

A large immigrant population has brought greater religious diversity than ever before, but the dominant religion is still Catholicism.

Café culture is a big part of life in Madrid

Culture

Many people come to Madrid just to walk the 'Golden Triangle' of its three world-class art museums: the Thyssen-Bornemisza, the Prado Museum and the Centro de Arte Reina Sofía. The latter is a collection of modern art and its star exhibit, Picasso's famous *Guernica*, is not to be missed. The other two museums, in contrast, have an abundance of old masters and you should allow plenty of time to visit both. While the Thyssen-Bornemisza is conceived as a tour of Western art in general, the Prado has an extraordinary collection of Spanish art. Its stars are two representatives of Spain's 17th-century 'Golden Age', when the Spanish empire was at the height of its glory: El Greco and Diego Velázquez. The Golden Age was also the time of writers, whose work has had an enormous influence on Spanish culture, particularly Miguel de Cervantes, the creator of *Don Quixote*, and the crazily prolific Félix Lope de Vega, who is said to have written 1,500 plays in his life. The fervour of the Golden Age also resulted in El Escorial, Felipe II's massive, sombre palace-monastery filled with art treasures.

Ironically, the Golden Age proved a turning point for Spain, after which it slipped into economic decline. Madrid took on a new cultural lease of life in the 18th century under the Bourbon dynasty of monarchs, who bequeathed it a wealth of art and architecture all heavily influenced by styles imported from France and Italy. The best example of this is the Palacio Real with its sumptuous interior decoration.

Not all art has to be grandiose, however, and Madrid has a secret cache of informal decoration to be seen in the elaborately tiled murals in its *tabernas*, old inns that mostly date from the 19th century.

🔺 *Literary heroes Don Quixote and Sancho Panza*

As for living culture, *madrileños* are proud of their theatrical tradition – but you'll need to understand Spanish to truly enjoy it. *Zarzuela* is another matter; this is Madrid's own form of operetta, an authentic expression of local culture, and even if you can't follow the storyline, at least you can enjoy the music.

THE MADRID CARD
The **Madrid Card** (☎ 902 08 89 08 🌐 www.madridcard.com) can be bought in advance online, or from various outlets in the city, and gives entry to 40 museums and other attractions; unlimited use of the Madrid Visión tourist bus (see page 54); and discounts at selected shops, restaurants and shows. It does not cover public transport.

Madrid has always been a melting pot for artists and musicians from all over Spain, drawn by the chance of making their reputations in the capital. Although it competes in some ways with Barcelona for the cream of the country's creativity, it is still a good place to see cutting-edge contemporary painting and sculpture, and to pick up new trends in Spanish music – there are an astonishing number of bars, often cramped and with tiny stages, where you can see up-and-coming musicians perform live.

Most successful internationally of all the arts has been Spain's flourishing film output. In this respect, Madrid's most famous son is the Oscar-winning Pedro Almodóvar, whose films are highly original and always riddled with a melodramatic dose of Spanish emotion, a provocative sense of humour and a reliably edgy cast of transvestites, prostitutes and other creatures of the night. His biggest hits include *Women on the Verge of a Nervous Breakdown*, *All About My Mother* and *Volver*.

● *The city hall, Plaza de Cibeles*

✔ MAKING THE MOST OF
Madrid

Shopping

Madrid has, alongside its chain stores and shopping centres, lots of old-fashioned, family-run specialist shops that exist mostly in the narrow backstreets of the Old Town. For more modern tastes, prowl around north of the **Gran Vía**, particularly in the Chueca and Malasaña districts, where there is a plethora of hip boutiques full of designer threads and homeware. For high-end shopping on spacious streets, try the glamorous district of **Salamanca**, where the ladies-who-lunch take their pocket dogs around the international designer boutiques.

One essential appointment is the famous flea market, **El Rastro**, which takes place on Sunday mornings (from about 07.00) in the streets around Calle Ribera de Curtidores – to get there, take the Calle de Toledo from the Plaza Mayor and turn left after the church of San Isidro. The stalls sell a mixture of antiques, household goods, second-hand items and a little of everything else. The real charm is the Rastro's bustling atmosphere rather than its bargain-hunting

● *Have a rummage at El Rastro flea market*

potential. Arrive early as the crowds build up towards noon – and at all times watch your bag.

If you just want a souvenir or present, make straight for one of Salamanca's shopping centres, such as ABC Serrano (see page 99), **El Jardín de Serrano** (ⓐ Calle de Goya 6–8 ⓣ 915 77 00 12 ⓦ www.jardindeserrano.es) or **Serrano 88** (ⓐ Calle Serrano ⓣ 914 26 35 88). And if you want to reduce the choice to one shop, make it El Corte Inglés (see page 66), the quintessential Spanish department store that strives to be a cut above in quality. The most convenient branch is the one adjacent to the Puerta del Sol.

USEFUL SHOPPING PHRASES

What time do the shops open/close?
¿A qué hora abren/cierran las tiendas?
¿A kay ora abren/theeyerran las teeyendas?

How much is this?	**Can I try this on?**
¿Cuánto es?	¿Puedo probarme esto?
¿Cwantoe es?	*¿Pwedo probarme esto?*

My size is (shoes) ...	**I'll take this one.**
Mi número es el ...	Me llevo éste
Mee noomero es el ...	*Meh llievo esteh*

This is too large/too small/too expensive. Do you have any others?
Es muy grande/muy pequeño/muy caro. ¿Tienen más?
Es mooy grandeh/mooy pekenio/mooy karo. ¿Teeyenen mas?

Eating & drinking

You'll rarely see locals eating as they walk along the streets in Madrid and that is because the rhythm of any *madrileño*'s day is marked by the delightful succession of stops for coffee, pastries, tapas, afternoon beers and, of course, the enormous lunch that marks the midway point. Not only is eating and drinking relatively cheap in the capital, it is also the perfect way to soak up the atmosphere and break up a hard day's sightseeing.

The city's huge number and variety of restaurants go by a number of different names, including *asador* (indicating that meat is roasted in a wood-fired oven), *mesón* and *tasca* (antiquated words for an inn). One speciality of Madrid is the *taberna*, an old bar that is often richly kitted out in ceramic tiles and invariably doubles as a restaurant. In all these places you'll find an ample selection of Spanish food, including the best of Basque cuisine (said to be the finest in the country) and the hearty specialities of Castile: roast suckling pig (*cochinillo asado*) and lamb (*cordero*). Surprisingly for a city so far from the coast, Madrid serves Spain's best selection of fish and seafood.

PRICE CATEGORIES

The price guides given when a restaurant is mentioned indicate the approximate price of a three-course meal (*menú del día* if there is one) for one person, excluding drinks, but including tax:

£ up to €20   ££ €20–40   £££ over €40

Ratings for cafés and bars are:

£ inexpensive   ££ moderately priced   £££ expensive

🔺 *Roasting suckling pig at Casa Botin*

If you're a dedicated carnivore and want to eat something truly local, then the only thing to order at midday in winter is Madrid's trademark stew, *cocido madrileño*, which is traditionally made in an earthenware crock (easy and cheap to buy if you want to try the recipe back home) and cooked over a wood fire. It is served in two parts: first comes the broth with fine pasta added to it; then the meat and vegetables. It is best accompanied by a strong red Spanish wine, like a bottle from La Mancha. You can eat a good *cocido madrileño* in many of the city's restaurants, and a few of them, such as La Bola (see page 69), offer little else by way of a menu. It should be added that Madrid has another, less glamorous, gastronomic speciality – tripe (*callos*).

If you don't care to sample local flavours, you'll also find lots of restaurants serving foreign food, particularly Latin American. As a vegetarian you'll survive the stay. Provincial Spain is not geared up for vegetarians at all, but Madrid has several dedicated vegetarian restaurants and even in a normal eatery most waiters will understand the concept of meat-free dishes.

Wherever you eat and whatever you order, the city's eating hours may take some getting used to. Lunchtime starts at 14.00 and you'll still get served at 16.00. Dinner is not until 21.00 at the earliest. A few tourist-friendly restaurants open earlier, but to eat anywhere authentic you'll need to adapt to this timetable.

The main meal in Spain is in the middle of the day and this is when most restaurants and *mesones* (taverns) offer a cheaper menu (*menú del día*), which typically consists of three courses with a bottle of the house wine thrown in. This is certainly the best way to fill up without spending a lot of money. But note that a *menú de degustación* is something altogether different. Only seen in high-class restaurants, it is a pricey sampler menu.

You're never far from a fast-food outlet; indeed, Spain has its own speed-eat – tapas. These can be nibbled at a bar counter or table at any time – simply request a *ración* if you want a larger portion.

Although Spain is generally weak on the old dessert menu, Madrid itself is strong on sweet snacks, and has excellent cake shops (*pastelerías*) that offer a little treat to go with a coffee.

Note that in more economical restaurants, you should put your knife and fork back on the table after finishing your first course as you will be expected to reuse them for the main dish.

Tipping is generally about 10 per cent in a restaurant; for a coffee or a drink at the bar, just round it up to the nearest euro or leave the change.

USEFUL DINING PHRASES

I would like a table for ... people
Quisiera una mesa para ... personas
Keysyera oona mesa para ... personas

Waiter/waitress!
¡Camarero/Camarera!
¡Camareroe/Camarera!

May I have the bill, please?
¿Podría traerme la cuenta por favor?
¿Pohdreea traherme la cwenta por fabor?

Could I have it well cooked/medium/rare please?
¿Por favor, la carne bien hecha/a punto/poco hecha?
¿Por fabor, la kahrrne byen echa/al poontoh/poecoh e cha?

I am a vegetarian. Does this dish contain meat?
Soy vegetariano. ¿Tiene carne este plato?
Soy begetahreeahnoh. ¿Teeyene carneh esteh plahtoh?

Where is the toilet (restroom) please?
¿Dónde están los servicios, por favor?
¿Donde estan los serbithios, por fabor?

I would like a cup of/two cups of/another coffee/tea
Quisiera una taza de/dos tazas de/otra taza de café/té
Keysyera oona tatha dey/dos tathas dey/otra tatha dey kafey/tey

Entertainment & nightlife

Madrid is world-famous for *la marcha* – the unstoppable party pulse that runs through the city after dark. Madrid acts like a magnet for the best acts from around Spain, and the climate allows you to be outdoors for much of the year, making it pleasant to waft between bars and clubs.

The golden rules are not to go out too early – certainly not before 23.00 – and to pace yourself by not drinking too much too quickly. Many people like to start the evening in a *bar de copas*, which serves only drinks (spirits mostly), often in slick style. They can be distinguished from everyday bars not only by their late opening hours but because they have few chairs, preened bar staff and loud music on the speakers, possibly controlled by a DJ. Only at 03.00 or so do people move on to the clubs – although be sure to call them *discotecas* because 'club' in Spanish sometimes has connotations of a roadside brothel.

Large, long-established, dependable discos include Joy Eslava (see page 72), Palacio Gaviria (see page 73) and the seven-storey behemoth Kapital (see page 89).

If you want to be entertained you'll find plenty of choice in Madrid. The theatre scene is vibrant and not every play is in Spanish – you'll occasionally find something in English or a mime. A better bet, however, is a musical. You might not understand the dialogue but you can still enjoy the songs – and you may even know the story already as there's been a trend of re-creating London- and Broadway-style hits for the Spanish market.

For something home-grown, you may want to consider seeing a *zarzuela*, or Spanish operetta, an art form that Madrid is particularly proud of – see the programme of the **Teatro de la**

🔺 *The Teatro Real, Madrid's opera house*

Zarzuela (🅐 Jovellanos 4 ☎ 915 24 54 00 Ⓜ Metro: Banco de España) –
or flamenco which comes from southern Spain but is brilliantly
performed in several venues in Old Madrid (see page 73).

For classical music, find out what's on at the **Auditorio Nacional
de Música** (🅐 Príncipe de Vergara 146 ☎ 913 37 01 40 Ⓜ Metro: Cruz
del Rayo). There are also many bars and cafés with a performer in
the corner, particularly at weekends.

Cinema is another option. Most films are shown dubbed in
Spanish but you can see English-language films (marked *versión
original* on adverts) at **Alphaville** (🅐 Martín de los Heros 14
☎ 915 59 38 36 Ⓜ Metro: Plaza de España), **Renoir** (🅐 Martín de
los Heros 12 ☎ 915 41 41 00 Ⓜ Metro: Plaza de España), **Filmoteca
Española Cine Doré** (🅐 Santa Isabel 3 ☎ 913 69 21 18 Ⓜ Metro:
Antón Martín) and the **Ideal Yelmo Cineplex** (🅐 Doctor Cortezo 6,
on Plaza Jacinto Benavente ☎ 913 69 25 18 Ⓜ Metro: Sol).

There are two casinos not far from Madrid. The closest, at
Torrelodones, heading towards La Coruña on the A6 motorway, is the
Casino Gran Madrid (☎ 900 90 08 10 Ⓦ www.casinogranmadrid.es). The
Gran Casino Aranjuez (☎ 902 39 30 30 Ⓦ www.grancasinoaranjuez.es),
as its name suggests, is at Aranjuez, 30 minutes south of Madrid off
the NIV motorway. It runs a free bus service from Madrid for clients.
If you are going to either casino, dress fairly smartly and take your
passport with you to show at the entrance.

To get anywhere within the city at night the best bet is to
take a taxi, although the metro runs conveniently late and starts
again at 06.00. There are also an efficient number of night buses
(nicknamed *buhos* or 'owls'), which run from a base at Plaza de
la Cibeles. However, some people would say that if you come
home before the metro starts operating you haven't had a full
night out.

◬ Dining late, by streetlight, is the norm in Madrid

Sport & relaxation

SPECTATOR SPORTS
Football

If you follow football, you'll already know that the sport is a near-religion in Spain and that *madrileños* divide themselves between the city's two first-division teams: the blisteringly successful Real Madrid and their lifelong and more erratic rivals, Atlético de Madrid. Real Madrid, popular throughout Spain, plays at the **Santiago Bernabeu stadium** (ⓐ Paseo de la Castellana 144 ⓣ 902 31 17 09 ⓦ www.realmadrid.es ⓜ Metro: Santiago Bernabeu), and even if you don't go to watch a match you can always visit the club's museum.

Bullfighting

There's another, more controversial, mass spectator event that you'll have to make your own mind up about. In society, on TV and in the

⬥ *Real Madrid's home stadium is the modern Bernabeu*

newspapers it's treated almost as an art form. You could condemn it as ritualised animal cruelty of the most cynical kind – and you'd find many Spaniards to support such a stance, particularly in the north of Spain where it is hardly practised at all – but there is no denying that it is a deeply embedded part of the culture. Madrid has one of the largest and most prestigious bullrings in the world – the neo-Moorish-style **Plaza de Toros de las Ventas** (ⓐ Alcalá 237 ⓣ 913 56 22 00 ⓦ www.las-ventas.com ⓜ Metro: Ventas). The season gets into its stride in May during the fiesta of San Isidro and lasts until October. *Corridas* are advertised in the press. You can buy tickets from the bullring's ticket office on the day but it is best to book in advance, especially if you want to sit in the shade (*sombra*) rather than bake in the cheaper sunny seats (*sol*).

PARTICIPATION SPORTS

The city has plenty of parks where you can walk, jog or kick a ball around. For swimming, try the pool in the **Casa de Campo** (ⓐ Avenida del Angel ⓣ 914 79 60 02 ⓛ Open all year ⓜ Metro: Lago), which also has a gym. There's skiing in season in the Guadarrama mountains north of Madrid and at any time of year in **Madrid Xanadú** (ⓐ Arroyomolinos, 23 km (14 miles) from central Madrid ⓣ 902 26 30 26 ⓦ www.madridxanadu.com), a shopping centre with Spain's only indoor ski slope.

RELAXATION

Head to the Acquaplaya spa baths in the **Hotel Senator España** (ⓐ Gran Vía 70 ⓣ 915 24 25 05 ⓦ www.hotelsenatorespana.com) or the hugely popular hammam **Medina Mayrit** (ⓐ Atocha 14 ⓣ 902 33 33 34 ⓦ www.medinamayrit.com), modelled on the Moorish baths found in Granada.

Accommodation

Although there are a growing number of mid-priced boutique hotels, Madrid is stronger by far on the two extremes of the hotel market. This means that you will have to compromise – either shell out for comfort or treat your accommodation as somewhere to sleep rather than hang around.

Hotels are officially ranked from one to five stars but this doesn't tell you much except the quantity of facilities; prices do not always correspond to stars. Generally cheaper are *hostales* (classified from one to three stars), which are not to be confused with youth hostels. *Hostales* can be guesthouses that often occupy the upper floors of an apartment block, have reduced facilities, are unlikely to have 24-hour reception or room service, occasionally do not have en-suite bathrooms and may not offer any meals apart from breakfast. *Pensiones* are also cheaper and more basic than hotels, but a well-cared for, family-run *pensión* or *hostal* can be a friendlier place to stay than a large modern hotel armed with all creature comforts.

Important points to look for when choosing a hotel in Madrid are location – walkable access to the sights and nightlife is a big advantage – and whether the rooms are soundproofed (if the place is on or near a busy street) and heated or air-conditioned, according

PRICE CATEGORIES

The price symbols indicate the approximate price of an en-suite room for two people for one night in high season, including tax:

£ up to €60   ££ €60–120   £££ over €120

to the season. Better hotels are located near the Paseo del Prado, near the Teatro Real in the Old Town and in the modern suburbs up the Paseo de la Castellana. For cheaper hotels, look along the Gran Vía, down Calle Atocha and in the districts of La Latina and Lavapiés south of the Old Town.

Booking a room is advisable if you are choosy about where you stay, and is essential in busy periods such as important trade fairs. Over the phone you will probably have to provide a credit card number to confirm the reservation. On arrival you will be asked to show your passport and may have to leave it at reception while the details are copied.

🔺 The elegant glass dome of the Palace Hotel

HOTELS & GUESTHOUSES

Benamar £ A well-located and friendly *hostal* divided into two parts. If possible, pay a little extra for the recently renovated part with en-suite bathrooms and PCs in every room. The older section is clean and adequate but has shared bathrooms. ⓐ San Mateo 20 (2nd and 3rd floors) ⓣ 913 08 00 92 ⓦ www.hostalbenamar.es ⓜ Metro: Alonso Martínez or Tribunal

Cervelo £ Very good value for central Madrid (very close to Puerta del Sol), with private bathrooms, air-conditioning and Wi-Fi access in the rooms. ⓐ Atocha 43 ⓣ 914 29 95 94 ⓦ www.hostalcervelo.com ⓜ Metro: Antón Martín

Horizonte £ A *hostal* founded in 1939 (the last year of the Civil War) and still run by the same family. Rooms are plain and simple, and the service unfailingly friendly and helpful. ⓐ Atocha 28 (2nd floor) ⓣ 913 69 09 96 ⓦ www.hostalhorizonte.com ⓜ Metro: Antón Martín

Carlos V ££ The great advantage of this classic hotel is its location close to the Puerta del Sol. Some rooms have terraces. Triple and quadruple rooms available. ⓐ Maestro Vitoria 5 ⓣ 915 31 41 00 ⓦ www.hotelcarlosv.com ⓜ Metro: Sol

Persal ££ Upmarket *hostal* with satellite TV, central heating, air conditioning and Wi-Fi access. Near the Plaza Santa Ana in the Old Town. ⓐ Plaza del Ángel 12 ⓣ 913 69 46 43 ⓦ www.hostalpersal.com ⓜ Metro: Sol or Antón Martín

Petit Palace Ducal Chueca ££ A comfortable boutique hotel in the Chueca district, off the Gran Vía, within a short walk of the main museums and other sights of the city. ⓐ Hortaleza 3 ☎ 915 21 10 43 ⓦ www.petitpalaceducalchueca.com Ⓜ Metro: Gran Vía

Adler Hotel £££ One of Madrid's most sophisticated boutique hotels, and a favourite among celebrities. It is located in the Salamanca district and surrounded by chic designer shops. ⓐ Calle Velázquez 33 ☎ 914 26 32 20 ⓦ www.adlermadrid.com Ⓜ Metro: Velázquez

De Las Letras £££ Built in 1917, this stylishly renovated luxury hotel has period statues, a hammam and a funky rooftop terrace. Excellent restaurant. ⓐ Gran Vía 11 ☎ 915 23 79 80 ⓦ www.hoteldelasletras.com Ⓜ Metro: Sevilla or Gran Vía

Palacio San Martín £££ A 19th-century palace converted into a luxurious hotel with courtyard, façade and stuccoed ceilings, and stunning views from the rooftop restaurant. ⓐ Plaza de San Martín 5 ☎ 917 01 50 00 ⓦ www.intur.com Ⓜ Metro: Sol

Petit Palace Puerta del Sol £££ The most central of this successful new chain of designer boutique hotels is right on the corner of the Puerta del Sol. Rooms are sleek with flat-screen TVs. ⓐ Arenal 4 ☎ 915 21 05 42 ⓦ www.hthotels.com Ⓜ Metro: Sol

Ritz £££ The classiest, most historic hotel in the city, charging correspondingly absurd prices. ⓐ Plaza de la Lealtad 5 ☎ 917 01 67 67 ⓦ www.ritzmadrid.com Ⓜ Metro: Banco de España

Room Mate Mario £££ Intimate, design-conscious hotel, well located for the sights of Old Madrid. ⓐ Campomanes 4 ☎ 915 48 85 48 ⓦ www.room-matehoteles.com Ⓜ Metro: Ópera

Villa Real £££ As luxurious as they come, this boutique hotel near the Prado reflects archaeologist owner Jordi Clos's interest in the Roman period. ⓐ Plaza de las Cortes 10 ⓣ 914 20 37 67 ⓦ www.derbyhotels.es ⓝ Metro: Sevilla or Sol

YOUTH & BACKPACKER HOSTELS

Barbieri International Hostel £ The best value for backpackers near the centre, in the trendy Chueca district. Reception and kitchen facilities are open 24 hours. ⓐ Barbieri 15 ⓣ 915 31 02 58 ⓦ www.barbierihostel.com ⓝ Metro: Chueca

MuchoMadrid £ Youth hostel with three mixed dormitories and one female dormitory. ⓐ Gran Vía 59 (7th floor) ⓣ 915 59 23 50 ⓦ www.muchomadrid.com ⓝ Metro: Plaza de España

CAMPSITES

Camping El Escorial Classy campsite 6 km (4 miles) from El Escorial with a large pool, restaurant, supermarket and nightclub. ⓐ Carretera El Escorial–Guadarrama ⓣ 902 01 49 00 ⓦ www.campingelescorial.com

Camping Osuna The closest campsite to the city centre, near a bus stop but not a metro. It's off the NII (Madrid to Barcelona motorway, at Km 8), heading towards Barajas town (not the airport). Services include a supermarket, laundry, restaurant, bar and live entertainment in the summer. ⓣ 917 41 05 10

⬥ *The contemporary interior of the Room Mate Mario hotel*

THE BEST OF MADRID

Madrid is a busy modern city with a medieval heart and a concentration of magnificent art galleries. It also has buzzing bars and cafés, great shops and a vibrant nightlife. All this and it makes a good base for day trips out to other places in central Spain.

TOP 10 ATTRACTIONS

- **Medieval Madrid** There's a maze of quaint old streets to explore heading south and west from the city's principal square of the Puerta del Sol. Particularly picturesque is the Plaza de la Villa halfway down the Calle Mayor (see page 60).

- **Plaza Mayor** This arcaded rectangle is at the heart of the Old Town, a place to stroll around or have a coffee in the sunshine (see page 63).

- **Palacio Real** The extravagantly ornate 18th-century royal palace of Spain (see page 62).

- **Museo del Prado** Spain's internationally famous collection of great art, with particular emphasis on Goya and Velázquez (see page 81).

- **Museo Thyssen-Bornemisza** This outstanding gallery across the road from the Prado offers a condensed tour through the history of Western art (see page 83).

- **Centro de Arte Reina Sofía** A superb collection of modern Spanish art, pride of place being reserved for Picasso's anti-war masterpiece *Guernica* (see page 79).

- **Parque del Retiro** The former grounds of a palace, Madrid's biggest park is a place to amble down tree-shaded avenues or go boating (see page 76).

- **El Escorial** The most popular day out from Madrid is to King Felipe II's massive palace-cum-monastery crammed with art (see page 112).

- **Bulls & football** Madrid has two favourite 'sports'. The city is at its most passionate during a *corrida* at Las Ventas bullring (see page 92) or a match of one of the city's two rival football teams, Real Madrid or Atlético (see page 32).

- **It's party time** Take time to enjoy Madrid's extraordinary number and diversity of *tabernas* (old-fashioned bars) and cafés, which blend into a sensational nightlife that goes on until dawn.

Plaza de Las Ventas is an icon of the Madrid horizon

Suggested itineraries

HALF-DAY: MADRID IN A HURRY
If you feel like walking, you can see the best of the Old Town in two or three hours, including some window-shopping and a coffee break. If it's winter or wet, you'll probably be better off going directly to the Prado, the Thyssen-Bornemisza or the Centro de Arte Reina Sofía.

1 DAY: TIME TO SEE A LITTLE MORE
A whole day in Madrid will give you a chance to relax over a leisurely lunch to break up the sightseeing. Half the day can be spent exploring the streets of the Old Town as outlined above and the other half in El Prado, the city's main art gallery. Take in a flamenco show in the evening.

2–3 DAYS: TIME TO SEE MUCH MORE
You'll be able to fit in El Prado and either the Reina Sofía or the Thyssen-Bornemisza galleries, along with a visit to the Palacio Real. Allow some time for wandering around the Old Town, visiting the Retiro Park and shopping in the Salamanca quarter. You could allocate one day for a trip out to El Escorial.

LONGER: ENJOYING MADRID TO THE FULL
As well as the three main art galleries and the Palacio Real, you'll have time to see lesser-known gems, such as the Monasterio de las Descalzas Reales or the Las Ventas bullring. Away from the Old Town, a stroll up the Paseo del Prado and the Castellana could easily fill a whole afternoon. Day trips might include El Escorial and at least one of the nearby monumental cities – Segovia (see page 128) and Toledo (see page 132) are closest.

REGE CAROLO III
ANNO
MDCCLXXVIII

⬥ The impressive Puerta de Alcalá is a useful landmark

43

Something for nothing

Prices in Madrid for everything from a T-shirt to a taxi have soared in recent years but it takes only a little knowledge and imagination to see how you can happily spend time in the city without needing wads of cash.

To begin with, there are atmospheric boulevards and squares to wander around, where the charm is in the buildings, monuments, statues and street life rather than in attractions you have to pay to get into. The best place to stroll is the Old Town and, in particular, if you don't want to be tempted by shops, La Latina quarter, southwest of the Plaza Mayor towards the Plaza de la Paja and Plaza de San Andrés. On Sunday mornings the streets of La Latina are occupied by the El Rastro street market (see page 22), which is almost more enjoyable to explore if you can't afford to buy anything. The busy Gran Vía is another interesting street to promenade along, mainly to look at its monumental buildings and shop windows.

When you get tired of streets, there are parks. The Retiro (see page 76) is the largest and most obvious but there are plenty more, some little frequented. Closest to the city centre are the Jardines de Sabatini (off the Plaza de Oriente), a raised terrace garden handy for a picnic.

Some public buildings are free to enter, including the cathedral and all churches (when they are open and a service is not being held), the two grand hotels – the Ritz (see page 37) and the Palace – the Senate and the Casa de América (see page 79). The **Museo de la Ciudad** (**ⓐ** Principe de Vergara 140 **ⓣ** 915 88 65 99 **Ⓝ** Metro: Cruz del Rayo) and the **Museo de Escultura al Aire Libre** (an outdoor sculpture museum **ⓐ** Paseo de la Castellano 41 **ⓣ** 917 01 18 63 **Ⓝ** Metro: Rubén Darío) are also free. The Prado (see page 81) is free Tuesday to Saturday

16.00–20.00 and on Sundays (🕐 17.00–20.00), on 2 May, 18 May (International Museum Day), 12 October and 6 December. The Centro de Arte Reina Sofía (see page 79) is free on Saturday afternoons and evenings from 14.30 to 21.00 and on Sunday mornings from 10.00 to 14.30 and on 18 April, 18 May, 12 October and 6 December. The partially open Museo Arqueológico Nacional (see page 80) is free on Saturdays from 14.30, on Sundays from 09.30 to 14.30 and on 18 May, 12 October and 6 December.

🔺 The Jardines del Retiro are a perfect way to pass a day for free

When it rains

From June to September, you shouldn't see much, if any, rain in Madrid but the rest of the year a shower or even a wet spell is more likely. If you are in the city only for the art, you probably won't mind what the weather's doing, but if you're hoping to spend most of your time strolling the streets, it's worth having a contingency plan (and getting familiar with the metro).

Obvious refuges for rainy days are any of the great museums, especially those where you can spend a protracted length of time, namely the Prado (see page 81), the Thyssen-Bornemisza (see page 83), the Reina Sofía (see page 79) and the Museo Arqueológico Nacional (see page 80). If you've run out of big museums, it could be an opportunity to visit one of the lesser-known ones, such as the **Museo del Romanticismo** (ⓐ San Mateo 13 ① 914 48 10 45 Ⓜ Metro: Tribunal), the Museo Lázaro Galdiano (see page 95) or the Museo de América (see page 94). Other indoor sights are the Palacio Real (see page 62), the iconic opera house, the **Teatro Real** (ⓐ Plaza Isabel II s/n ① 915 16 06 60), and the former convent, now art museum, the **Monasterio de las Descalzas Reales** (ⓐ Plaza de las Descalzas Reales 3).

Or you could get some shopping done. Department stores (especially El Corte Inglés; see page 66) and shopping centres such as those in the Salamanca district (see page 99) are suitable shelters.

If you haven't got the energy to shop, any atmospheric *taberna* or café – such as the Café Gijón (see page 87), the **Café Comercial** (ⓐ Glorieta de Bilbao 7 ① 915 21 56 55 Ⓜ Metro: Bilbao), the Café de Oriente (see page 69) or the Café del Círculo de Bellas Artes (see page 86) – will make a relaxing nook to linger over a coffee. Another good place for a rainy-day coffee, or just to sit, is the old

Atocha Station, which has been turned into a giant hothouse kept at an even temperature of 24°C (75°F).

If you want to forget the weather, you might want to indulge yourself in the hammam on Calle Atocha or spend a whole day undercover at the new giant ice rink, bowling alley, shopping centre and cinema complex of the **Palacio de Hielo** (ⓐ Silvano 77 ❶ 902 20 29 30 Ⓦ www.palaciodehielo.com Ⓝ Metro: Canillas). Or you could even take a bus out to Madrid Xanadú (see page 33) and spend the day skiing and shopping, oblivious to what it's like out of doors.

🔺 *The venerable Café de Oriente*

On arrival

TIME DIFFERENCE

Spain follows Central European Time (CET). The clocks go forward one hour in late March.

ARRIVING

By air

National and international flights arrive at Madrid's airport, **Aeropuerto de Barajas** (ⓐ Avenida de la Hispanidad ☏ 902 40 47 04 ⓦ www.aena.es) 12 km (7 miles) northeast of the centre.

The quickest way to get into the city is to take a taxi from an official rank (outside Terminals 1, 2, 3 and 4) – don't go with one of the touts who may approach you inside the airport. It's a 20-minute journey except during rush hour and should cost around €20, not including the airport supplement (or the luggage supplement).

Your other option is the metro. You can take line 8 (coloured pink on the maps) directly from terminals 1, 2 and 3 (it's not so convenient for terminal 4); this takes you to Nuevos Ministerios Station in about 12 minutes and from here you can change on to line 10 (coloured navy blue), which will take you down to Plaza de España. To get to Sol you'll need to change again at Plaza de España to get Line 3 (coloured yellow). For timetables, see ⓦ www.metromadrid.es

Alternatively, take bus number 200, which runs between terminals 1 and 2 and the Avenida de América metro station. The service runs from 05.20–23.30 and buses leave every 16–20 minutes; the journey takes around 45 minutes, depending on traffic. Tickets can be bought on board. Of the six stops en route, the one at Avenida de América metro station is probably the best connected. Bus number 204 offers the same service from terminal 4.

By rail

Trains from the north of Spain arrive at the **Estación de Chamartín** (ⓐ Agustín de Foxa) and those from the east and south, including the high-speed AVE from Córdoba and Seville, arrive at the **Estación de Atocha** (ⓐ Plaza Emperador Carlos V). For all train information, contact ⓣ 902 24 02 02 ⓦ www.renfe.es. Both stations are on the metro but Atocha is much closer to the centre, right opposite the Reina Sofía museum.

By road

If you arrive by coach, you will probably be dropped off at **Estación Sur de Autobuses** (ⓐ Méndez Alvaro 83 ⓣ 914 68 42 00/914 68 45 11 ⓦ www.estacionautobusesmadrid.com ⓜ Metro: Méndez Alvaro) to

◆ *One of Madrid's beautiful ceramic street signs*

the south of Madrid city centre. It's next to the metro (line 6), and bus number 148 runs from here to central stops such as Plaza de España and Plaza Callao. Note that taxis charge a small supplement (€3) to carry passengers from the bus station. If the coach is not international or long-distance, the company you are travelling with may have its own private bus terminal elsewhere in the city.

Madrid traffic can be a shock to the unaccustomed. If you have to drive into Madrid, it's best to have a secure parking place lined up and head straight for it, but be prepared to pay through the nose. Avoid rush hours (07.30–09.00 and 19.00–20.30) and driving in the twisting streets of the Old Town. If there is a quieter time to be driving in the city, it is during the lunch break, around 15.00–16.00.

FINDING YOUR FEET

Madrid is a lively, busy cosmopolitan city where surprisingly few people you will meet will claim to be long-term residents. Many of them will have migrated here from other parts of Spain, other European countries or from Latin America or North Africa. In some cases Spanish may be their second language and the city as unfamiliar as it is to you. In the tourist-trodden parts of the city English is widely understood and spoken.

Inevitably, Madrid has its criminals on the lookout for easy prey. You should have no problems if you always keep your bag and camera close to you and don't stop to look at your map in a dark alley. Pickpocket hotspots are the most touristed and crowded parts of town, particularly the Plaza Mayor and the Puerta del Sol.

ORIENTATION

It's worth spending your first hour or so in the city becoming familiar with the layout, especially before you plunge into the streets of the

Old Town. You can't mistake the conspicuous north–south axis formed
by the Paseo del Prado, Paseo de Recoletos and Paseo de la Castellana,
which connects the two railway stations of Atocha and Chamartín.
East–west, your line of reference is the Gran Vía and Calle de Alcalá
from the Plaza de España in the west to the Parque del Retiro in the
east. In the Old Town the Puerta del Sol and the Plaza de Oriente are
the best places to return to if you get lost. In extremis, head for the
nearest metro station and take a train to Sol Station (for the Puerta
del Sol), which is on lines 1, 2 and 3.

IF YOU GET LOST, TRY ...

Excuse me, do you speak English?
Perdone, ¿habla usted inglés?
Perdoneh, ¿ahbla oosted eengless?

**Excuse me, is this the right way to the Old Town/the city
centre/the tourist office/the station/the bus station?**
Perdone, ¿por aquí se va al casco antiguo/al centro de
la ciudad/a la oficina de turismo/a la estación de trenes/
a la estación de autobuses?
*Perdoneh, ¿por akee seh ba al kasko anteegwo/al thentroe dey
la theeoodad/a la offeetheena dey toorismoe/a la estatheeon
dey treness/a la estatheeon dey owtoebooses?*

Can you point to it on my map?
¿Puede señalármelo en el mapa?
¿Pwaydeh senyalarmayloe en el mapa?

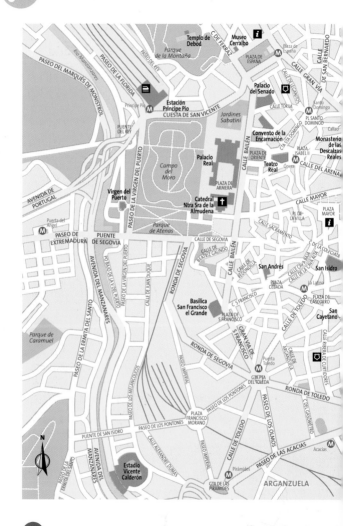

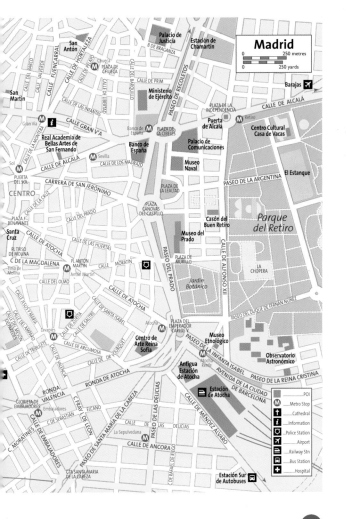

Madrid

| 0 | | 250 metres |
| 0 | | 250 yards |

Palacio de Justicia
Estación de Chamartín
B DE BRAGANZA
San Antón
Chueca PLAZA DE CHUECA
CALLE DE PRIM
CALLE FUENCARRAL
CALLE DE HORTALEZA
CALLE DEL BARCO
CALLE VALVERDE
CALLE DE LIBERTAD
CALLE DE LAS INFANTAS
Ministerio de Ejército
PASEO DE RECOLETOS
Barajas ✈
San Martín
PLAZA DE LA INDEPENDENCIA
CALLE DE ALCALÁ
Gran Vía
Calle GRAN VÍA
CALLE DE LA MONTERA
Banco de España
PLAZA DE LA CIBELES
Puerta de Alcalá
Retiro
Centro Cultural Casa de Vacas
Real Academia de Bellas Artes de San Fernando
Sevilla
Banco de España
Palacio de Comunicaciones
Sol
PUERTA DEL SOL
CALLE DE ALCALÁ
CALLE DE LOS MADRAZO
Museo Naval
El Estanque
CENTRO
CARRERA DE SAN JERÓNIMO
PASEO DE LA ARGENTINA
CALLE DE LA CRUZ
PLAZA DE LA LEALTAD
Parque del Retiro
PLAZA J. BENAVENTE
CALLE DEL PRADO
PLAZA CÁNOVAS DEL CASTILLO
Santa Cruz
CALLE DE ATOCHA
CALLE DE LAS HUERTAS
Casón del Buen Retiro
PL TIRSO DE MOLINA
PLANTÓN MARTÍN
CALLE MORATÍN
Museo del Prado
CALLE DE ALFONSO XII
C DE LA MAGDALENA
Tirso de Molina
Antón Martín
PLAZA DE MURILLO
LA CHOPERA
CALLE DEL OLMO
CALLE DE ATOCHA
Jardín Botánico
CALLE DE JESÚS Y MARÍA
CALLE DE SANTA ISABEL
PASEO DEL DUQUE DE FERNÁN NÚÑEZ
CALLE DEL MESÓN DE PAREDES
CALLE DEL AMPARO
CALLE DE LA FE
CALLE DE SALITRE
Lavapiés
Atocha
PLAZA DEL EMPERADOR CARLOS V
Museo Etnológico
Observatorio Astronómico
CALLE DE TRIBULETE
CALLE DE ARGUMOSA
CALLE DE DR. FOURQUET
Centro de Arte Reina Sofía
PASEO DE LA INFANTA ISABEL
PASEO DE LA REINA CRISTINA
Antigua Estación de Atocha
Atocha Renfe
AVENIDA DE LA CIUDAD
CALLE DE VALENCIA
RONDA DE ATOCHA
Estación de Barcelona
RONDA VALENCIA
GLORIETA DE EMBAJADORES
C FRAY DE LEÓN
ELCANO
PASEO DE LAS DELICIAS
CALLE DE MÉNDEZ ÁLVARO
Estación de Atocha
Embajadores
C DE SEBASTIÁN
CALLE DE LAS DELICIAS
C. MORATINES
CALLE DE EMBAJADORES
PASEO DE SANTA MARÍA DE LA CABEZA
La Sepulvedana
CALLE DE ANCORA
GTA SANTA MARÍA DE LA CABEZA
CALLE DE RAFAEL DE RIEGO
Estación Sur de Autobuses

■	POI
Ⓜ	Metro Stop
✝	Cathedral
🛈	Information
🚓	Police Station
✈	Airport
🚂	Railway Stn
🚌	Bus Station
✚	Hospital

53

GETTING AROUND

The best way to get from sight to sight is on foot. In the Old Town you have no other option, and the major monuments and museums are all within walking distance of each other. If you get tired or want to get to places beyond the immediate centre, the metro is more convenient than buses, which are slowed by the traffic, but for a short hop a bus will be the best bet. For several or frequent journeys on public transport, buy a Metrobús ticket, which gives you ten trips by bus or metro and is cheaper than individual tickets. They are on sale in metro stations, tobacconists (*estancos* marked with a Tabacos sign outside) and newsstands (*kioskos*). Taxis are handy, especially in the wider modern streets.

Madrid's underground system, the metro, is cheap and usually fast. There are 13 lines (including the new Metrosur and Ramal lines), although you'll probably make most use of the central ones: 1 (blue), 2 (red) and 3 (yellow). Stations are well indicated at street level by a horizontal diamond logo framed in red. Trains run from 06.00 to 02.00 and run (depending on the line) every 3–5 minutes on weekdays and about every 10–15 mins after 23.00 and on Sundays. Despite constant promises from the city council, the metro still does not provide an all-night service on Saturdays. For more information ❶ 902 44 44 03 Ⓦ www.metromadrid.es

One way to get to know the city quickly is to take a **Madrid Visión** hop-on hop-off tourist bus (❶ 917 79 18 88 Ⓦ www.madridvision.es) with a multilingual recorded commentary. The open-top double-decker buses run around two routes: Historic Madrid, including the Palacio Real and Plaza de España (with stops at the Museo del Prado, Plaza Cibeles, Museo Arqueólogico and Puerta de Alcalá), and Modern Madrid (along the Gran Vía and the Paseo del Prado). For go-as-you-please freedom on buses and the metro, a Tourist Travel Pass is valid for 1, 2, 3, 5 or 7 days' unlimited use; available from the same outlets as the Madrid Card (see page 20).

Bus services are efficient except when the traffic snarls up during rush hours, and the metro is often easier to use for newcomers to the city. The most useful bus routes for sightseeing are: Line 2, stopping at Plaza de España, goes along Gran Vía to Cibeles and Retiro Park; Line 3 goes from the Puerta de Toledo up Gran Vía de San Francisco and Calle Mayor to the Puerta del Sol; Line 5 goes from Puerta del Sol past Cibeles, Plaza de Colón and up the Paseo de la Castellana to Chamartín. When you get on a bus you can either pay the driver for the journey (although they are not obliged to give you change for large notes) or insert your Metrobús card in the machine near the entrance.

⬤ *La Calle de Alcalá is the most major thoroughfare of Madrid*

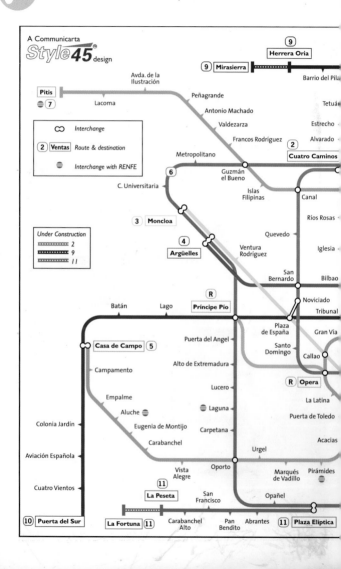

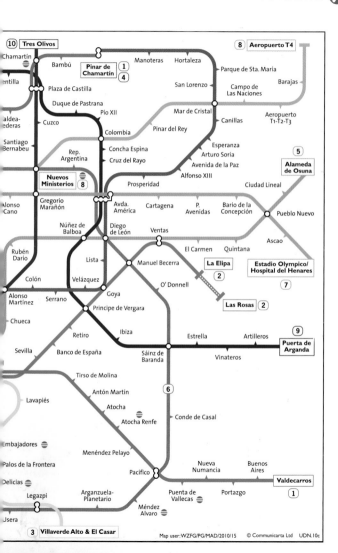

Map user:WZFG/PG/MAD/2010/15   © Communicarta Ltd   UDN.10c

Taxis, conspicuously white, are easily hailed on any main street and are not too costly. But they can easily get stuck in gridlock. A green light means a taxi is for hire. The fare will be fixed by meter, which may start at a minimum charge. Tariffs increase at night and if you have luggage, and there is also an extra fee for airport transfers. For a pickup, call **Radio Taxi** ☎ 914 05 55 00 or **Tele Taxi** ☎ 913 71 21 31.

Madrid's traffic jams are notorious and it's not worth trying to drive around the city unless you particularly want to. Most of the Old City is pedestrianised and should be avoided altogether in a car. In addition, car parks and parking spaces can be hard to find. If you have arrived by car, it is best to leave it parked in a hotel garage or secure car park and explore on foot, or by public transport or taxi.

CAR HIRE

When hiring a car you will need to show your passport and EU or international driving licence. All the major car hire companies have offices in Madrid but you can usually get the best deal by reserving a car from home at the same time as making a flight booking. The following companies have offices at Barajas airport:

Avis ☎ 902 13 55 31 Ⓦ www.avis.es

Hertz ☎ 917 49 77 78 Ⓦ www.hertz.es

National/Atesa ☎ 902 10 01 01 Ⓦ www.atesa.es

Other companies with offices in Madrid are:

Europcar ☎ 902 10 50 30 Ⓦ www.europcar.es

Spaincar ☎ 902 22 46 46 Ⓦ www.spaincar.es

▶ *The towers of the Ermità de la Virgen del Puerto*

THE CITY OF
Madrid

Old Madrid

This tangle of narrow medieval streets south of the Gran Vía is the first port of call for most first-time visitors to Madrid. Here the streets are boiling over with atmosphere, whatever the time of day. The area has plenty of historic buildings but it is also thick with little shops, bars and cafés, and has a concentration of good restaurants and clubs too.

The only way to get around here is on foot. The natural place to begin is the elongated square, the Puerta del Sol, which is regarded not only as the centre of Madrid but of Spain as well. From here, it's a short hop to the handsome Plaza Mayor and the quaint Plaza de la Villa, and not much further to the Catedral de la Almudena. Next door is the magnificent royal palace, the Palacio Real, which stands at the top of the steep slope down to the river, thus marking the abrupt west end of the Old Town.

SIGHTS & ATTRACTIONS

Gran Vía
A look skywards on this busy street, thronging with roaring traffic, high-street shops and restaurants, reveals some interesting early 20th-century architecture, notably the Edificio Metrópolis (at the junction with Calle de Alcalá), the Edificio Grassy (on the corner with Calle Caballero de Gracia) and the Telefónica building, which looks like a scaled-down Manhattan skyscraper. ⓜ Metro: Gran Vía

Plaza de la Villa
On Madrid's most attractive monumental square stands the 17th-century Ayuntamiento (city hall) connected to the 16th-century Casa de Cisneros by an arch. The most interesting building on the square

Old Madrid

POI
Metro Stop
Cathedral
Information
Police Station
Railway Stn
Bus Station

Banca de España

CALLE DEL BARQUILLO

GRAN VIA

CALLE DE LAS INFANTAS

Real Academia de
Bellas Artes de
San Fernando

CALLE DE ALCALÁ

CALLE DE LOS MADRAZO

CALLE DE ZORRILLA

CALLE DE CERVANTES

CALLE LOPE DE VEGA

CALLE DE SANTA ISABEL

CALLE DE SANTA CATALINA

CALLE DE ATOCHA

CARRERA DE SAN JERÓNIMO

VENTURA DE LA VEGA

CALLE DE LAS HUERTAS

PL ANTÓN
MARTÍN

CALLE DE
ECHEGARAY
PRÍNCIPE
PL SANTA ANA
INFANTE

CALLE DEL PRADO

Antón Martín

CALLE DEL OLMO

AVE. MARÍA

CALLE DE

CALLE DE LA MAGDALENA

CALLE DE LA CABEZA

OLIVAR

CALLE DE LAVAPIÉS

CALLE JESÚS Y MARÍA

CALLE DEL AMPARO

CALLE DEL MESÓN
DE PAREDES

Lavapiés

San Martín

CALLE GRAN VÍA
Gran Vía

CALLE DE LA MONTERA

CALLE DEL CARMEN

CALLE DE PRECIADOS

M PEZ

M FDEZ
GONZÁLEZ
VICTORIA

PUERTA
DEL SOL

PIE MATEHU

PLAZA DE
BENAVENTE

PZA DEL
ÁNGEL

CALLE CAÑIZARES

Tirso de Molina

CALLE DE LA CONCEPCIÓN JERÓNIMA

San Martín

CALLE CONCHAS

Santo
Domingo

PL SANTO
DOMINGO

CALLE DE LAS HILERAS

Callao

CALLE SAN MARTÍN

CALLE DE LAS DESCALZAS
REALES

Monasterio
de las
Descalzas
Reales

PZA DE LAS
DESCALZAS

PZA SAN
GINÉS

Ópera

CALLE MAYOR

Sol

CENTRO

Santa Cruz

PLAZA
MAYOR

Opera

SAN FELIPE
NERI

PLAZA DE
ISABEL II

PZA
ISABEL II

CALLE DE LA COLEGIATA

San Isidro

CUCHILLEROS

PLAZA DE
SAN MIGUEL

CALLE DE LA CAVA BAJA

CALLE CAVA ALTA

CALLE DUQUE DE ALBA

CALLE ENCOMIENDA

CALLE DE LA ESCUADRA

San Millán y
San Cayetano

CALLE RIBERA DE

CALLE DE CURTIDORES

La Latina

CALLE DE TOLEDO

Convento de
la Encarnación

Teatro
Real

C CONDE
DE LEMOS

PLAZA DE
ORIENTE

PLAZA DE
VILLA

CONDE DE
MIRANDA

CALLE DEL CORDÓN

C. SACRAMENTO

Palacio
del Senado

CALLE TORIJA

CUESTA DE SANTO DOMINGO

CALLE REYES

Jardines
Sabatini

CALLE BAILÉN

CALLE SAN NICOLÁS

San Andrés

PLAZA DE
ATAZANA

PLAZA DE LA
PAJA

GONZÁLEZ

CALLE BAILÉN

PLAZA DE
S. FRANCISCO

CALLE DE SEGOVIA

Palacio
Real

PLAZA DE
ARMERÍA

Catedral
Ntra Sra de la
Almudena

Campo
del Moro

CUESTA DE SAN VICENTE

Estación
del Norte

Príncipe
Pío

PASEO DE LA VIRGEN DEL PUERTO

Virgen del
Puerto

Parque
de Atenas

CALLE DE SEGOVIA

Basílica
San Francisco
el Grande

RDA DE SEGOVIA

CALLE DE AGUILA

CALLE DE LOS YESEROS

CALLE SANTA ANA

PASEO DE LA VIRGEN DEL PUERTO

CALLE DE JARDINES SEGOVIA

CALLE DE JUAN DUQUE

N

0   500 metres
0   500 yards

① ② ③ ④ ⑤ ⑥ ⑦ ⑧ ⑨ ⑩

is the 15th-century Torre de los Lujanes, with its Gothic portal
and Mudéjar horseshoe arches. The statue in the middle of the
square by Benlliure is of Alvaro de Bazán, hero of the naval battle
of Lepanto, a key Spanish victory in 1571 against the Ottoman Turks.
Ⓜ Metro: Ópera or Sol

PALACIO REAL

Spain's Bourbon monarchs took the remarkably short period
of 28 years to build themselves this royal palace in the 18th
century. It remained occupied by the royal family until 1931,
when Republican crowds forced King Alfonso XIII to abdicate.
Later, Franco used it for state business and its balcony as a
platform from which to give speeches. The current king of
Spain, Juan Carlos I, lives in the Palacio de la Zarzuela and the
Palacio Real is now open to the public except when it is needed
for state ceremonial occasions.

Inside, the palace is all excessive ornamentation, the
particular highlights of which are: a throne room draped in
scarlet velvet and gold embroideries; the Gasparini rooms,
named after their Neapolitan interior designer, and lavishly
decorated in embroidered silk, stucco and complementary
furniture; and a room entirely walled in figured porcelain.

Next to the palace, the gardens of the Campo del Moro slope
gracefully downhill towards the Río Manzanares. But you will
need to walk a little to their separate entrance on Paseo de la
Virgen del Puerto. ⓐ Calle Bailén ⓣ 914 54 88 00 ⓛ 09.30–17.00
Mon–Sat, 09.00–14.00 Sun, closed for state functions Ⓜ Metro:
Ópera or Plaza de España ⓘ Admission charge

◔ *The magnificent Palacio Real*

Plaza Mayor

If the Puerta del Sol is Madrid's functional main square, its official and ceremonial public space is the neatly rectangular Plaza Mayor. It's often used for fiestas, outdoor theatre, political rallies and other public events; formerly it hosted bullfights and the Inquisition's *autos-da-fé*. In the middle of the square stands King Felipe III mounted on his horse and on one side is the Casa de la Panadería, a building painted with somewhat garish allegorical murals. It's a good place to flee from the traffic and people-watch from the café terrace tables, particularly at night, when legions of buskers, street masseurs and artists come out to entertain you. ◔ Metro: Sol

Puerta del Sol

This square (really more of a stretched half-moon shape, criss-crossed by traffic) is the natural place to begin a walking tour of Old Madrid and a good place to return to when you need to get your bearings or hop into a taxi. You certainly couldn't get more central than this, where a plaque set into the pavement under the clock tower of the Casa de Correos marks *kilómetro cero*, the point from which all Spain's road distances are measured. On the rounded side of the square is *El Oso y El Madroño*, a statue of a bear eating the foliage of a strawberry tree, the symbol of the city of Madrid and a time-honoured meeting place.

The Puerta del Sol seems always to have been at the centre of events. Here the trams began their first journeys, the city's first street lamps were installed and the first metro station was built. This is the square portrayed in Goya's masterpiece, *El dos de mayo*, which depicts the slaughter of the *madrileños* by Napoleon's Mameluke cavalry in 1808. A short-lived constitution was proclaimed in the square in 1812 and the first Republic in 1873. More gruesomely, Franco had his enemies imprisoned in the cells of the Ministry of the Interior, which occupied the building forming the straight side of the square.

The Puerta del Sol comes into its own on New Year's Eve, when the nation's TV cameras train on the crowds gathered for the traditional eating of the 12 grapes to the chimes of the clock (see page 11).
Ⓝ Metro: Sol

CULTURE

Monasterio de las Descalzas Reales
There is a superb art collection hidden behind the somewhat stern façade of this 16th-century convent (of the 'royal barefoot nuns'), which was founded by Juana de Austria, the sister of Felipe II. Over the staircase is a *trompe l'œil* fresco of Felipe IV and his family on a balcony. The rest of the art is presented in a series of chapels off a cloister and includes works by Titian, Rubens, Zurbarán and Breughel.
ⓐ Plaza de las Descalzas Reales 3 ❶ 914 54 88 00 ❶ 10.30–12.45,

16.00–17.45 Tues–Thur & Sat, 10.30–12.45 Fri, 11.00–13.45 Sun
Ⓝ Metro: Sol or Callao ❶ Admission charge

Museo de la Real Academia de Bellas Artes de San Fernando

This academy, founded in 1794, is considered to be Spain's third most
important collection of historical art after the Museo del Prado and
the Thyssen-Bornemisza, and has the virtue of being less well known
and therefore less busy. The 1,300 paintings on display are of varying
interest. Spanish artists such as Juan de Juanes, Ribera, Zurbarán,
Murillo, Velázquez and Sorolla are all here but they are eclipsed by
the collection of Goya's work, which includes two self-portraits and
his Carnival picture, *The Burial of the Sardine*. ⓐ Calle de Alcalá 13
(off Calle Gran Vía) ❶ 915 24 08 64 🕐 09.00–17.00 Tues–Sat,
09.00–14.30 Sun Ⓝ Metro: Sevilla or Sol ❶ Admission charge

RETAIL THERAPY

Antigua Casa Talavera A well-stocked shop specialising in traditional
Spanish ceramics, all sourced from independent Spanish producers.
ⓐ Isabel la Católica 2 (off Calle Gran Vía) ❶ 915 47 34 17 🕐 10.00–13.30,
17.00–20.00 Mon–Fri, 10.00–13.30 Sat Ⓝ Metro: Santo Domingo

El Arco de Cuchilleros Has a range of swords, fans and other traditional
crafts from all over Spain. ⓐ Plaza Mayor 9 ❶ 913 65 26 80
🕐 11.00–20.00 Mon–Sat Ⓝ Metro: Sol

Area Real Madrid Sells T-shirts and anything and everything else
emblazoned with the club's logo. There is another branch near
Bernabeu football stadium. ⓐ Calle del Carmen 3 ❶ 915 21 79 50
🕐 10.00–20.45 Mon–Sat, 11.00–18.45 Sun Ⓝ Metro: Sol

El Corte Inglés Spain's leading chain of department stores has two branches in Old Madrid and others in the city. ➌ Preciados 3 & Princesa 42 ➊ 913 79 80 00 ◷ 10.00–22.00 Mon–Sat Ⓝ Metro: Sol or Gran Vía

El Flamenco Vive An excellent range of music, books, clothes, shoes, guitars and everything else to do with flamenco. ➌ Conde de Lemos 7 ➊ 915 47 39 17 ◷ 10.30–14.00, 17.00–21.00 Mon–Sat Ⓝ Metro: Opera

Fnac Sells books, DVDs and a large range of CDs of Spanish music, as well as Cuban and Latin American dance tracks. It also sells concert tickets and develops photographs. ➌ Preciados 28 ➊ 915 95 61 00 ◷ 10.00–21.30 Mon–Sat Ⓝ Metro: Sol or Gran Vía

Guitarrería F Manzanero This guitar maker's workshop is the real thing if you are interested in buying an instrument. ➌ Calle Santa Ana 12 ➊ 913 66 00 47 ◷ 10.00–13.30, 17.00–20.00 Mon–Fri (winter); 10.00–13.30 (summer) Ⓝ Metro: La Latina

Mercado de San Miguel A pretty 19th-century pale green wrought-iron façade surrounds this lively market with a café in the centre. Stalls sell fresh produce, including olives and cured meats, and it's a great place to pick up essentials for a picnic in Retiro Park or to listen to a concert. ➌ Plaza de San Miguel Ⓦ www.mercadodesanmiguel.es ◷ 10.00–24.00 Mon, Tues, Wed & Sun, 10.00–02.00 Thur–Sat Ⓝ Metro: Sol

El Riojano Do as the royal family do and buy your teatime cakes in this charming old *pastelería*. Among its specialities are *azucarillos*, which dissolve in water to flavour it. There is a tearoom in the back.

ⓐ Calle Mayor 10 ⓣ 913 66 44 82 ⓛ 10.00–14.00, 17.00–21.00
Mon–Sat; 10.00–14.30, 17.30–21.00 Sun ⓜ Metro: Sol

Sanatorio de Muñecos The oldest toyshop in Madrid, the 'doll hospital'
fixes broken toys and is also packed with beautifully crafted traditional
toys. ⓐ Preciados 21 ⓣ 915 21 04 47 ⓛ 10.00–20.00 Mon–Sat ⓜ Metro: Sol

TAKING A BREAK

Chocolatería San Ginés £ ❶ Popular with hungry clubbers and
shoppers alike, the most famous *chocolatería* in town has been serving
up gloopy hot chocolate and plates of *churros* (deep-fried sticks of
batter covered in sugar) since 1894. Pay and take your ticket before
you sit down. ⓐ Pasadizo de San Ginés 5 ⓣ 913 65 65 46
ⓛ 09.30–07.00 daily ⓜ Metro: Ópera or Sol

Museo del Jamón £ ❷ A chain of dependable, no-nonsense tapas
bars where the décor is formed by hundreds of suspended legs
of *jamón serrano* (cured ham). Guess what's on the menu? Not
a place for vegetarians. ⓐ Calle Mayor 7 ⓣ 915 31 45 50 ⓛ 13.00–16.30,
20.30–24.00 ⓦ www.museodeljamon.com ⓜ Metro: Sol

Café del Real ££ ❸ Stop off for *café con leche* and a slice of
chocolate cake at this cosy, wood-beamed café stuffed with red
leather armchairs and old opera posters. ⓐ Plaza de Isabel II
ⓣ 915 47 21 24 ⓛ 09.00–01.00 Mon–Thur, 10.00–02.30 Fri & Sat,
closed Sun ⓜ Metro: Ópera

Gula Gula ££ ❹ 'Greedy greedy' serves up fast food in the form of a
hot and cold buffet at midday, and a salad bar and hot dish at night,

🔺 A barquillero, *wafer-seller, in the Plaza de Oriente*

but everyone's eyes are on the floor show of oiled waiters prancing about in tight leather shorts. Evening floor shows. 🄰 Calle Gran Vía 1 🄣 915 22 87 64 🄛 13.00–16.30, 21.30–23.30 Mon–Wed & Sun, 13.00–16.30, 21.30–02.30 Thur–Sat 🄽 Metro: Gran Vía

Café de Oriente £££ 🄹 An elegant café and restaurant facing the Palacio Real. Have a meal or a drink at one of the old-fashioned brass-rimmed tables to watch well-dressed people come and go. 🄰 Plaza de Oriente 2 🄣 915 47 15 64 🄛 08.30–01.30 Mon–Thur, 08.30–02.30 Fri & Sat, 09.00–01.30 Sun 🄽 Metro: Ópera

AFTER DARK

RESTAURANTS
Artemisa £ 🄺 Madrid's best-known vegetarian restaurant dishes up big, creative salads and a good taster menu. No smoking. 🄰 Ventura de la Vega 4 🄣 914 29 50 92 🄛 13.30–16.00, 21.00–24.00 daily 🄽 Metro: Sevilla

Viuda de Vacas £ 🄻 The battered refectory tables and red curtains may look familiar to fans of Pedro Almodóvar, who has used it as a film set on more than one occasion. A family-run affair, the food is good Castilian home cooking such as baked bream or stuffed aubergines. 🄰 Cava Alta 23 🄣 913 66 58 47 🄛 13.30–16.30, 21.00–24.00 Mon–Wed, Fri & Sat, 13.30–16.30 Sun 🄽 Metro: La Latina

La Bola Taberna ££ 🄼 Dating from 1870, and long renowned for its piping-hot crocks of *cocido madrileño* cooked over a wood fire. 🄰 Bola 5 🄣 915 47 69 30 🄛 13.00–16.00 Mon & Sun, 13.00–16.00, 20.30–23.30 Tues–Sat 🄽 Metro: Ópera or Santo Domingo

Casa Botín ££ ❾ In business since 1725, this is supposedly the oldest restaurant in the world and a star stop on Madrid's Hemingway route. Its speciality is suckling pig roasted in a wood-fired oven, but the lamb is also superb. ❸ Cuchilleros 17 ❶ 913 66 42 17 ⓦ www.botin.es ❸ 13.00–16.00, 20.00–24.00 daily ❽ Metro: Sol

Lhardy ££ ❿ Ironically, this old-fashioned French restaurant is one of the best places to eat the typical local dish of *cocido madrileño*, although you'll pay a high price for it. The shop on the ground floor is worth a look. ❸ Carerra de San Jerónimo 8 ❶ 915 21 33 85 ⓦ www.lhardy.com ❸ 13.00–15.30, 20.30–23.00 Mon–Sat, 13.00–15.30 Sun ❽ Metro: Sol

BARS

Café del Español This smart bar next to the Teatro Español sports chandeliers and red velvet banquettes, which makes the apple tart and coffee seem just a little bit more special. ❸ Príncipe 25 ❶ 913 60 14 84 ❸ 12.00–01.00 Mon–Wed & Sun, 12.00–02.00 Thur, 12.00–03.00 Fri & Sat ❽ Metro: Sol or Antón Martín

Cervecería Alemana This 1904 bar is as popular now as it was in regular Ernest Hemingway's time, although its fame makes it slightly touristy. Spanish and imported beers served. ❸ Plaza Santa Ana 6 ❶ 914 29 70 33 ❸ 10.00–00.30 Sun–Thur, 10.30–02.00 Fri & Sat ❽ Metro: Sol or Antón Martín

Las Cuevas del Sésamo A fabulously atmospheric basement bar that's so popular for the first drink of the evening that there's often a queue down the street to get in. There's also live piano music every night except Monday at about 21.00. ❸ Príncipe 7

🕿 914 29 65 24 🕒 19.00–02.00 Mon–Thur, 19.00–02.30 Fri & Sat
🔵 Metro: Sevilla or Sol

De 1911 Grab one of the coveted pavement tables at this diminutive bar for some heady cocktails, and a mix of traditional and modern tapas. 🅰 Plazuela San Ginés 5, corner of Calle Coloreros 🕿 913 66 35 19 🕒 18.00–01.30 Mon–Thur, 18.00–03.00 Fri & Sat

La Venencia This ancient, no-frills sherry den still chalks up orders on the bar and serves up manchego cheese and chorizo sausage for those who want something to go with their *fino* or *oloroso*. 🅰 Echegaray 7 🕿 914 29 73 13 🕒 13.00–15.00, 19.30–01.30 daily 🔵 Metro: Sevilla

Viva Madrid A well-known Old Madrid *taberna* off Plaza de Santa Ana transformed into a modern drinking spot. Worth visiting for its exterior

🔺 *Hemingway's old haunt in the narrow streets west of the Prado*

and interior tilework alone. Manuel Fernández y González 7
🕐 914 29 36 40 🕐 13.00–02.00 Mon–Thur & Sun, 13.00–03.00 Fri
& Sat Ⓜ Metro: Sevilla or Antón Martín

LIVE MUSIC

Café Central Considered Spain's most stimulating jazz club, with
live music from 10.00 to 24.00 and a cover charge (reduced Mon).
Ⓐ Plaza del Angel 10 🕐 913 69 41 43 Ⓦ www.cafecentralmadrid.com
Ⓜ Metro: Tirso de Molina or Antón Martín ① Admission charge

Café Jazz Populart This bar near Plaza de Santa Ana focuses on Spanish
and international jazz, plus some blues and fusion. Ⓐ Huertas 22
🕐 914 29 84 07 Ⓜ Metro: Antón Martín ① Admission charge

Museo Chicote This Art Deco restaurant and cocktail bar puts
on both live music and DJs at night. Legends such as Hemingway,
Ava Gardner and Grace Kelly have partied here. Ⓐ Gran Vía 12
🕐 915 32 67 37 Ⓦ www.museo-chicote.com Ⓜ Metro: Gran Vía

Oba-Oba For over a quarter of a century, Oba-Oba has been the
place to go for a taste of Brazil. Knock back a stiff *caipirinha* and
enjoy the live samba. Ⓐ Jacometrezo 4 🕐 No phone Ⓜ Metro: Callao
① Admission charge

CLUBS

Joy Eslava This former theatre is frequented by Madrid celebs
(and tourists). It's open nightly till 06.00 and, although it's more
expensive at weekends, you can usually pick up a flyer in a hotel
giving you discounted admission. It's worth reserving a table.
Ⓐ Arenal 11 🕐 915 66 37 33 Ⓜ Metro: Ópera ① Admission charge

Palacio Gaviria An 1850s, Italian Renaissance-style mansion a club? You bet, and there are also dance classes, exhibitions and cabarets. ⓐ Arenal 9 ☏ 915 31 26 01 🕓 Daily Ⓜ Metro: Sol ⓘ Admission charge

FLAMENCO SHOWS

Flamenco music and dance originate from southern Spain but Madrid has several restaurants where you can see a good show with dinner. A cheaper alternative is to buy a ticket that includes a drink but not a meal.

Café de Chinitas A famous flamenco venue graced in the past by the likes of Princess Diana and Bill Clinton. Dinner and the show come at a steep price. ⓐ Torija 7 (near Plaza de Santo Domingo) ☏ 915 59 51 35 Ⓦ www.chinitas.com Ⓜ Metro: Santo Domingo ⓘ Admission charge

Las Carboneras A touristy, fun, sexy flamenco joint: who needs authenticity? ⓐ Plaza Conde de Miranda 1 ☏ 915 42 86 77 Ⓦ www.tablaulascarboneras.com Ⓜ Metro: Sol

Casa Patas A highly reputed dinner-and-show flamenco venue, which attracts some big names in the flamenco scene. ⓐ Cañizares 10 (off Calle de Atocha in Lavapies) ☏ 913 69 04 96 Ⓦ www.casapatas.com Ⓜ Metro: Antón Martín ⓘ Admission charge

Corral de la Morería Hemingway, Che Guevara and Picasso have all been entertained here in the past. The pricey entrance ticket includes dinner. ⓐ Morería 17 ☏ 913 65 84 46 Ⓦ www.corraldelamoreria.com Ⓜ Metro: La Latina ⓘ Admission charge

THE CITY

The Cultural Quarter

Between the Old Town and the Parque del Retiro is a strip of the city sometimes referred to as Bourbon Madrid after the dynasty of monarchs that developed it in the 18th century. This is the place to lose yourself in three sensational museums that no art lover should miss. Foremost among them is the Museo del Prado, a repository of great paintings with an accent on home-grown Spanish talent. Across the road is the Thyssen-Bornemisza, which provides a methodical summary of Western art. In complete contrast is the Centro de Arte Reina Sofía, distinct from the other two geographically and thematically, where all the art belongs squarely to the 20th and 21st centuries.

These three galleries are linked by the broad boulevard of the Paseo del Prado. For a break, plunge into the spacious Retiro Park for shady tree-lined promenades, pools and fountains.

SIGHTS & ATTRACTIONS

Jardín Botánico

On a hot day there is nothing as refreshing as a stroll around Madrid's lush botanical gardens, situated just by the Prado Museum. Containing over 30,000 plant species, the gardens were yet another bequest of that tireless improver, King Carlos III. They were designed by Juan de Villanueva with the aid of botanist Gómez Ortega in 1781. ➌ Plaza de Murillo 2 ➊ 914 20 30 17 ⌚ 10.00–18.00 (Oct–Feb); 10.00–19.00 (Mar); 10.00–20.00 (Apr & Sept); 10.00–21.00 (May–Aug) Ⓜ Metro: Atocha ➊ Admission charge

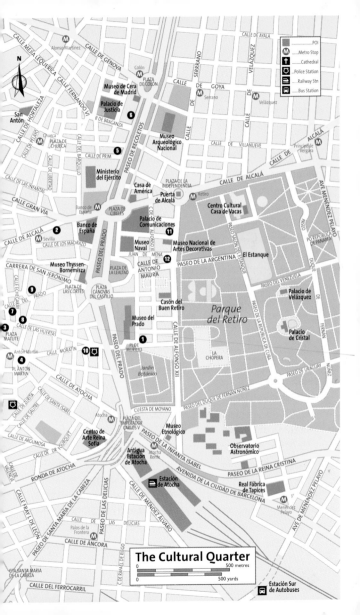

The Cultural Quarter

	POI
Ⓜ	Metro Stop
✝	Cathedral
☆	Police Station
⊖	Railway Stn
🚌	Bus Station

0 — 500 metres
0 — 500 yards

THE CITY

Parque del Retiro

Behind the Prado Museum is Madrid's favourite park, formerly the grounds of a palace occupied by Felipe IV. Its layout is fairly regular and in the middle is a large lake, El Estanque, which acts as a reference point. Miniature naval battles were once staged here for the amusement of royalty but it is now used for pleasure boating. Go southeast and you should find the unusual sculpture of *El Ángel Caído* (*The Fallen Angel*), by Ricardo Bellver, in one of the park's crossroads.

The park is also the home of the neoclassical Observatorio Astronómico and two art exhibition spaces, the **Palacio de Cristal** (☏ 915 74 66 14), inspired by London's Crystal Palace, and the brick and tile **Palacio de Velázquez** (☏ 915 73 62 45), named after the architect Ricardo Velázquez; both act as annexes for the Reina Sofía art museum and hold excellent temporary shows. The nearby **Centro Cultural Casa de Vacas** (☏ 914 09 58 19) is another exhibition space run by Madrid City Council. A good way to leave the park is down the sloping Cuesta de Moyano, lined with second-hand bookshops, which delivers you to the southern end of the Paseo del Prado. Ⓜ Metro: Retiro

Paseo del Prado

This attractive and stately avenue runs north–south from Atocha Station up to Cibeles, Madrid's unofficial symbol: a fountain with a statue in the middle named after Cybele, the Roman goddess of fertility and natural abundance. Originally called the Salón del Prado (*prado* means 'meadow'), it was commissioned in the 18th century by Carlos III to emulate the great avenues of Paris and was dotted with fine statues and fountains and lined by centres of culture and learning. The effect has been rather ruined by years of heavy and polluting traffic, and plans are currently under way to pedestrianise the central section.

🔺 El Ángel Caído, *Retiro Park*

◯ *The massive statue in the Plaza de Cibeles*

Walking down the Paseo del Prado you soon come to the semicircular **Plaza de la Lealtad** (on your left), which adjoins the **Plaza Cánovas del Castillo** – popularly known as *Neptuno* (Neptune) because of the fountain in the centre. Grouped around these two squares are: the stock exchange, the Museo Thyssen-Bornemisza and Madrid's two grand hotels facing each other, the Ritz and the Palace (both good places for a coffee if you want to rub shoulders with visiting VIPs). Just off the squares, going up Carrera de San Jerónimo, is Spain's Parliament, the Congreso de los Diputados.

Continuing down the Paseo del Prado, the newly expanded Museo del Prado is on your left followed by the 18th-century royal botanic gardens, where there are over 30,000 types of flora on terraces and in a hothouse. The boulevard ends in another broad roundabout, the Plaza del Emperador Carlos V, on which stands Atocha Station.

Puerta de Alcalá

Carlos III had this ceremonial gateway designed by Francesco Sabatini and erected in 1778 at what was then the eastern boundary of the city. Nowadays, it stands in the middle of a spacious traffic island. It's a useful landmark and looks particularly good when floodlit at night. ⓐ Plaza de la Independencia Ⓝ Metro: Retiro

CULTURE

This area of town, with virtually back-to-back museums, is where culture vultures will want to spend the majority of their time.

Casa de América

The 'House of America' occupies the beautiful Palacio de Linares and holds an interesting collection of Latin American art. It promotes Latin culture and hosts films, theatre, music and talks by prominent speakers. The terrace holds arts events in the summer months.
ⓐ Palacio de Linares, Paseo de Recoletos 2 ⓣ 915 95 48 00
Ⓦ www.casaamerica.es ⓛ 11.00–20.00 Mon–Sat, 11.00–15.00 Sun
Ⓝ Metro: Banco de España

Centro de Arte Reina Sofía

Many visitors to this museum come mainly to see what is arguably the most famous painting of the 20th century, Pablo Picasso's *Guernica* – but there is plenty more here. The building itself is an 18th-century hospital ingeniously adapted to its present use by the attachment of two glass lift shafts, designed by British architect Ian Ritchie, to the façade. The rear of the building has recently been expanded, with three glass and steel buildings by Jean Nouvel, housing temporary exhibitions, a library and an auditorium.

The gallery is on four floors, the first and third for temporary exhibitions, and the second and fourth devoted to the permanent collection: 'historical' modern art and contemporary work respectively. The emphasis throughout is on Spanish art.

One room is dedicated to the bizarre and often provocative work of Salvador Dalí, although here you can also see a more 'normal' side to his work. Another Surrealist, the film-maker Luis Buñuel who collaborated with Dalí, also gets a room.

Inevitably, though, it is Picasso who draws the crowds. *Guernica* is as large in reputation as it is in size. Intended as a mute expression of the absurdities of war, it has been described as one of the few political paintings that works artistically. The subject is a bombing raid on the Basque town of Guernica by Nazi pilots in support of General Franco on 26 April 1937. ⓐ Calle de Santa Isabel 52 ⓣ 917 74 10 00 ⓦ www.museoreinasofia.es ⓒ 10.00–21.00 Mon, Wed–Sat, 10.30–14.30 Sun ⓝ Metro: Atocha ⓘ Admission charge (free Sat pm & Sun am)

Museo Arqueológico Nacional

You can get a good sense of Spain's history in this archaeological treasure trove where the pick of the country's vast finds, from early prehistory to the 19th century, is kept. The earliest exhibits include three statues of *damas* (ladies) named after their places of origin. The Roman occupation of the Iberian Peninsula and the medieval period are well covered, and there are sections explaining the short-lived Visigothic era and the far-reaching influence of the Islamic civilisation of Spain. The building is currently undergoing major refurbishment, but part of it is kept open to exhibit a changing selection of the museum's best arefacts. ⓐ Serrano 13 ⓣ 915 77 79 12 ⓦ www.man.es ⓒ 09.30–20.00 Tues–Sat, 09.30–15.00 Sun ⓝ Metro: Serrano

THE BEST OF SPANISH ART AT THE PRADO

One of the world's greatest art collections, the **Museo del Prado**, just got even more impressive following the unveiling of its new extension. Designed by Rafael Moneo, the extension has increased the site by a whopping 50 per cent and allowed an overhaul of some of the more cramped galleries, including the museum's biggest crowd-puller, the Velázquez rooms.

The collection is still mostly housed in the neoclassical Palacio de Villanueva, built in 1785 on the orders of Carlos III, and is particularly strong on Spanish art. If you haven't got time to explore it all, head for the sections on the country's two most famous artists, Velázquez and Goya.

The treasures of El Prado came originally from the Spanish royal family and now include 8,600 paintings, as well as over 5,000 drawings, 2,000 etchings, almost 1,000 coins and medals, 700 Greek and Roman sculptures, and assorted furniture, tapestries and precious objects. The most interesting pieces of the collection are on show, with most space given to paintings, and all are organised by date and country of origin.

The galleries on the ground floor (*planta baja*) cover mainly Spanish, Flemish and Italian art up to the 16th century. A highlight is Hieronymus Bosch's three-panelled *The Garden of Earthly Delights* (c. 1516), a sermon against the deadly sin of lust. Another painting to look out for is Fra Angelico's *The Annunciation* (c. 1430), which depicts the Angel Gabriel telling the Virgin Mary that she has been chosen to be the Mother of Jesus. Other important artists represented are Botticelli, Pieter

Brueghel the Elder, Albrecht Dürer, Titian and Rubens. There are also some works by El Greco who, although born in Crete, spent most of his life in Spain, but you'll see much more of his work in Toledo (see page 132), where he lived and worked.

The first floor (*planta primera*) concentrates mostly on the 17th century. In Spain this period is known as the Golden Age and its leading artists were José de Ribera, Francisco Ribalta and Francisco de Zurbarán, but above all Diego de Velázquez (1599–1660). El Prado has almost all the important works painted by Velázquez, who became court painter to Felipe IV. His masterpiece is widely considered to be *Las Meninas* (1656), which includes a self-portrait of the artist painting the painting.

The other outstanding figure of Spanish art, Francisco de Goya (1746–1828), was influenced by Velázquez and also served as court painter. His work is renowned for its expressiveness, its humanity and occasionally its ambiguity. Two of his most famous works, *The Clothed Maja* and *The Naked Maja*, hang side by side. Another interesting Goya painting is *The 3rd of May*, which shows events in 1808 when Napoleon's troops had occupied Spain; on the day in question, French soldiers executed Spanish patriots in Madrid. The central figure in the painting has his arms raised in a Christ-like posture, a gesture to which Picasso refers in his *Guernica*. ❸ Paseo del Prado ❶ 913 30 28 00 ❷ www.museodelprado.es ❸ 09.00–20.00 Tues–Sun ❷ Metro: Atocha or Banco de España ❶ Admission charge (free 18.00–20.00)

⬥ The Prado is one of the world's great art museums

Museo Nacional de Artes Decorativas

The National Museum of Decorative Arts has five floors of tapestries, tiling, sculpture, porcelain, furniture and woodcarving. There are many Chinese pieces but most of the collection is Spanish and the standout piece is on the fifth floor, where an 18th-century kitchen has been lifted tile by tile from a Valencian palace. ⓐ Montalbán 12 ⓣ 915 32 64 99 ⓦ http://mnartesdecorativas.mcu.es ⓛ 09.30–15.00 Tues–Sat, 10.00–15.00 Sun ⓜ Metro: Banco de España or Retiro ⓘ Admission charge (free on Sun)

Museo Thyssen-Bornemisza

As if El Prado wasn't enough, across the street is the 18th-century Palacio de Villahermosa, home to a now expanded version of what was originally industrialist Baron Heinrich Thyssen-Bornemisza's personal collection of Western art. Begin on the top floor and work your way down the building anticlockwise to discover the development of European painting through almost seven centuries, starting with Italian art and moving through Flemish, German, Spanish and French painting. Highlights on the top floor include: the diptych *The Annunciation* by Jan Van Eyck; *Our Lady of the Dry Tree* by Petrus Christus; the famous portrait of Henry VIII by Hans Holbein; Raphael's *Portrait of a Young Man*; *Jesus Among the Doctors* by Dürer; *St Jerome in the Wilderness* by Titian; and Rubens' *The Toilet of Venus*.

The first floor takes the story from Dutch 17th-century painting to German Expressionism passing through Impressionism and Post-Impressionism: Manet, Monet, Degas, Renoir, Sisley and Van Gogh are all here. By the ground floor you have reached the 20th century, represented by Picasso's *Harlequin with a Mirror*, Lucien Freud's *Portrait of the Baron Thyssen-Bornemisza* and Edward Hopper's *Hotel Room*. The museum's holdings have been newly extended with the Carmen Thyssen-Bornemisza collection, housed in the two adjoining buildings (at Nos 19 and 21 of Calle Marqués de Cubas, accessed from Room 18 on the second floor) and containing some 300 works belonging to the late baron's wife, 'Tita'. The collection includes works by Constable, Van Gogh, Degas, Renoir and Rodin. ❸ Paseo del Prado 8 ❶ 913 69 01 51 Ⓦ www.museothyssen.org ❷ 10.00–19.00 Tues–Sun ❷ Metro: Banco de España ❶ Admission charge

Palacio de Comunicaciones

An outrageously over-the-top wedding cake of a building that seems somewhat overblown for its role as the city post office. Designed in 1904 by Antonio Palacios and Joaquín Otamendi, it is a glamorous swirl of marble, columns, staircases and Art Nouveau flourishes. It also contains the **Museo Postal y Telegráfico**

(🚇 entrance on Calle Montalbán ☎ 913 96 20 00) with its vast
stamp collection and displays showing the history of Spanish
mail from post horns to the Hispasat satellite. 🏛 Plaza de Cibeles
☎ 917 40 06 68 🕐 09.00–14.00, 16.00–18.00 Mon–Fri
🚇 Metro: Banco de España

Real Fábrica de Tapices

Before he went on to lampoon the royal family with his famously
mocking portraits, Goya worked as a cartoonist at the royal tapestry
factory, which continues to produce his designs today. In his day
the factory, founded in 1721, was located in Chueca, but it has been
at its current site for well over a century and continues to restore
and create tapestries for the royal palace and the Ritz hotel, among
others. Call ahead to arrange an English-speaking guide as tours
are usually in Spanish. 🏛 Fuenterrabía 2 ☎ 914 34 05 50 🕐 Guided
tours only 10.00–14.00 Mon–Fri 🚇 Metro: Menéndez Pelayo
ⓘ Admission charge

RETAIL THERAPY

There aren't many shops in this part of Madrid and for a classier type
of gift you may find museum shops the most interesting places to
browse. For kitschy souvenirs, head to the street stalls and shops at
the top of the Paseo del Prado near the entrance to the Prado Museum.

Casa Mira A delightful old *pastelería* selling a range of home-made
chocolates, pastries, marzipans, candied fruits and *turrones* (Spain's
favourite Christmas treat made from almonds). 🏛 Carrera de San
Jerónimo 30 ☎ 914 29 88 95 🕐 10.00–14.00, 16.30–21.00 Mon–Sat,
10.30–14.30, 17.30–21.00 Sun 🚇 Metro: Sevilla

Desnivel Adventurers and travellers can find a huge selection of books, guides and maps covering Spain and other lands. The owners are also a mine of information about local walking groups and good hiking trails. ⓐ Plaza Matute 6 ❶ 902 24 88 48 ⓦ www.libreriadesnivel.com ⓛ 10.00–14.00 & 16.30–20.30 Mon–Sat Ⓝ Metro: Antón Martín

TAKING A BREAK

El Botánico £ ❶ For a coffee and snack after the Prado, avoid the tourist-thronged cafés on the Paseo del Prado and head around the back of the museum instead. This café serves up hot buttered baguettes for breakfast, with tapas and a set lunch later in the day. ⓐ Ruiz de Alarcón 27 ❶ 914 20 23 42 ⓛ 08.30–24.00 Ⓝ Metro: Banco de España

Café del Círculo de Bellas Artes £ ❷ Watch street life from the windows of this café in Madrid's much-loved fine arts centre. There is a small admission fee if you're just having coffee but entrance is now free for clients who wish to stop for lunch. With its painted ceilings but arty clientele, it feels like an old-fashioned gentlemen's club without the stuffiness. ⓐ Alcalá 42 ❶ 913 60 54 00 ⓛ 09.00–13.00 Mon–Thur & Sun, 09.00–03.00 Fri & Sat Ⓝ Metro: Banco de España or Sevilla

Casa Alberto £ ❸ The décor is as ancient as the waiters at this atmospheric old *taberna*. There are classic tapas out front, a restaurant in the back and a trough of running water at the bar to keep the wine cool. ⓐ Huertas 18 ❶ 915 21 07 06 ⓛ 11.00–01.30 Tues–Sat Ⓝ Metro: Antón Martín

Cine Doré £ ❹ (Filmoteca Española) You might catch an English-language film at Spain's national film theatre, or simply graze in the café soaking up its understated arty atmosphere. ❸ Santa Isabel 3 ❶ 913 69 11 25 ❷ Metro: Antón Martín

Café Gijón ££ ❺ One of the few legendary cafés to survive into the 21st century, the Gijón is redolent of the great literary and intellectual discussions that took place here before the Civil War. Nowadays, it is a haven for quiet conversation. There is a restaurant downstairs. ❸ Paseo de Recoletos 21 ❶ 915 21 54 25 ❷ Metro: Colón or Banco de España

El Pabellón del Espejo ££ ❻ This eye-catching pavilion on Paseo de Recoletos is a refreshing place for a drink, tapas or an inexpensive meal. ❸ Paseo de Recoletos 31 ❶ 913 08 23 47 ❷ Metro: Colón

🔺 *The historic Café Gijón*

AFTER DARK

RESTAURANTS

El Cenador del Prado ££ ❼ Gourmet Spanish cuisine from the Herranz brothers dished up in style. Try the vegetarian taster menu and superlative desserts. ⓐ Calle de Prado 4 ❶ 914 29 15 61 ⓦ www.elcenadordelprado.com ❶ 13.45–15.45, 20.45–23.45 Mon–Sat ⓝ Metro: Antón Martín

Come Prima ££ ❽ Gourmet Italian cuisine served up in a light and airy Tuscan-themed dining room. It's one of the few places in the city where you can get a real risotto – and everyone knows it – so be sure to book in advance. ⓐ Echegaray 27 ❶ 914 20 30 42 ❶ 21.00–24.00 Mon, 13.30–16.00, 21.00–24.00 Tues–Sat ⓝ Metro: Antón Martín

Ølsen ££ ❾ The second of the deservedly successful string of Ølsens, Leticia Saharrea's formula of glamour, superlative Nordic cuisine, warm wood interiors and exotic vodka menu make for a wonderful night out. The Belvedere Lounge plays late-night deep house and lounge on Fridays and Saturdays. ⓐ Calle del Prado 15 ❶ 914 29 36 59 ⓦ www.olsenmadrid.com ❶ 13.00–17.00, 20.00–02.00 Mon–Thur & Sun, 13.00–17.00, 20.00–02.30 Fri & Sat ⓝ Metro: Sevilla

La Vaca Verónica ££ ❿ Charming if stridently decorated restaurant serving a menu strong on meat and fish, spaghetti and salads. ⓐ Moratín 38 ❶ 914 29 78 27 ❶ 14.00–16.00, 20.30–00.30 Mon–Sat, 14.00–16.00 Sun ⓝ Metro: Antón Martín

Horcher £££ ⓫ Leave your high-fashion threads at the door: this restaurant is strictly old-school. The menu, strong on game and backed by an impressive wine list, is international with an accent on Central Europe, reflecting the Horcher family's roots. Reserve ahead and dress smartly. ⓐ Calle de Alfonso XII 6 ⓣ 915 22 07 31 ⓦ www.restaurantehorcher.com ⓛ Closed Sat lunch, Sun & Aug ⓝ Metro: Retiro

Viridiana £££ ⓬ Named after a film by the Surrealist Luis Buñuel, this gastronomic temple to cinema will perfectly round off a day spent in the art galleries. Order the *menú de degustación* if you can't decide what to have. ⓐ Juan de Mena 14 ⓣ 915 23 44 78 ⓦ www.restauranteviridiana.com ⓛ Closed Sun ⓝ Metro: Banco de España or Retiro

CLUBS
Discoteca Azúcar The perfect place to dance to salsa, rumba, merengue and other Caribbean rhythms. Dance classes are available if you need them. Tropical cocktails are served. ⓐ Paseo Reina Cristina 7 ⓣ 915 01 61 07 ⓝ Metro: Atocha

Kapital A massive club occupying a seven-storey building. The main dance floor plays house; the third and fourth floors are designated a 'soul area' with R&B and funk; and the fifth floor serves up pop, salsa and oldies. There's much more going on apart from dancing, including karaoke and various other entertainments. If you want to slow down for a while, the seventh floor is a relaxing terrace. No trainers. ⓐ Calle de Atocha 125 ⓣ 914 20 29 06 ⓛ Until 06.00 Thur, Fri & Sat ⓝ Metro: Atocha ⓘ Admission charge

Northern Madrid

By the 1800s, Madrid was hopelessly overcrowded so building work began on the *ensanche* (expansion) of the city to the north and the east of the Gran Vía, the Plaza de Colón and the Puerta de Alcalá. With its orderly grids and wide avenues, this large area of the city holds some amazing architecture, world-class shopping and lesser-known museums.

The central axis of northern Madrid is the brash, modern highway of the Paseo de la Castellana, lined with futuristic office buildings, which takes off from the Plaza de Colón and ends a short way beyond the Estación de Chamartín railway station.

Immediately accessible by foot from Old Madrid, however, are the districts of Malasaña, Conde Duque and Chueca, a bohemian and studenty cluster of streets around the Plaza Dos de Mayo and the Plaza de Chueca. They make good hunting grounds for hip bars, ethnic restaurants and interesting little shops.

The Beckhams may have left town but the bling lives on in the wealthy and incurably *pijo* (sloaney) Salamanca district on the other side of the Paseo de la Castellana. Along its wide streets, laid out on a grid, you'll find fashionable shops specialising in big-name brands.

Northern Madrid has several appealing museums, among them the eccentric Lázaro Galdiano (see page 95). They are fairly spread out and you'll need to hop between them by metro, bus or taxi.

SIGHTS & ATTRACTIONS

Ermita de San Antonio de la Florida

This deconsecrated chapel has superb frescoes painted by Goya in 1798, notably one showing the Miracle of St Anthony, in which the

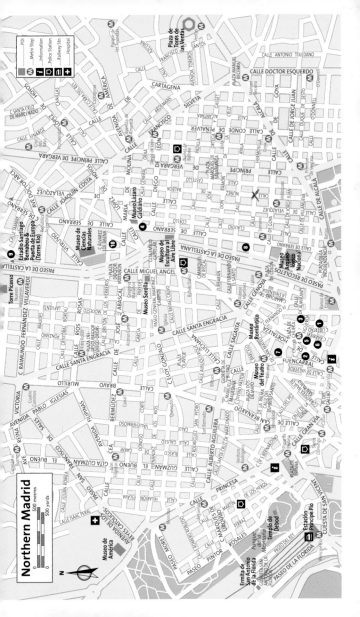

PASEO DE LA CASTELLANA

Any notion that Madrid is merely a city of past glories is dispelled instantly by a bus or taxi ride up this uncompromisingly modern central avenue lined with the tower blocks of Spain's biggest corporations. It starts at Plaza de Colón as a continuation of the Paseo del Prado and Paseo de Recoletos, and finishes over 5 km (3 miles) later. Approximately halfway up is the Azca complex of shops and offices above which looms the 157 m (515 ft) Torre Picasso, the tallest building in Madrid. Across the road diagonally from Azca is Real Madrid's home ground, the Estadio **Santiago Bernabeu**.

Towards the top end of the Castellana is the extraordinary **Puerta de Europa** (or Torres Kio), which consists of two 120 m (390 ft) high towers leaning towards each other at a spectacular angle over the Plaza Castilla.

saint brings a dead man back to life surrounded by angels, street beggars and priests. ⓐ Glorieta San Antonio de la Florida 5 ⓣ 915 42 07 22 ⓒ 10.00–20.00 Tues–Fri, 10.00–14.00 Sat & Sun ⓝ Metro: Príncipe Pío

Plaza de Toros de las Ventas

Madrid's bullring was built in 1931 in neo-Mudéjar style (derived from Islamic architecture) with horseshoe arches around the galleries. It can hold 20,000 spectators. There are guided tours (ask at the ticket office) but it is far better to see a bullfight during the season between May and October. At any time you can visit the museum, Museo Taurino (ⓣ 917 25 18 57), which has exhibits illustrating

the history of bullfighting. 🅰 Calle de Alcalá 237 ☎ 913 56 22 00
🕐 09.30–14.30 Mon–Fri (Nov–Feb); 09.30–14.20 Tues–Fri,
10.00–13.00 Sun (Mar–Oct) Ⓝ Metro: Ventas

Templo de Debod
This Egyptian temple was built by Adijalamani in the fourth century
BC and given to Spain by Egypt as a tribute to Spanish engineers
who helped save ancient monuments from the rising waters of the
Aswan Dam. It forms the centrepiece of the Parque de la Montaña.
Its carved reliefs show Amen, god of fertility and life. At the far end,
there are spectacular views over the Palacio Real and the Campo del
Moro gardens. 🅰 Calle Ferraz ☎ 917 65 10 08 🕐 09.45–13.30, 16.15–18.00

🔺 *The gravity defying Puerta de Europa*

● *The Templo de Debod in the Parque de la Montaña*

Tues–Fri; 10.00–14.00 Sat & Sun ◉ Metro: Ventura Rodríguez
❶ Admission charge

CULTURE

Museo de América

This museum explores the relationship between the old and new worlds, particularly Spain and its former colonies. Its exhibits, including many pre-Columbian treasures from the Olmecs, Toltecs, Maya and other vanished civilisations, are organised into five themes: the discovery of America, present-day Latin America, religion (both indigenous and imported), writing and language. One of its most important artefacts is the treasure of the Quimbayas, a collection of gold pieces donated by the Colombian government. ⓐ Avenida de los

Reyes Católicos 6 ☎ 915 49 26 41 🌐 http://museodeamerica.mcu.es
🕐 09.30–15.00 Tues–Sat, 10.00–15.00 Sun Ⓜ Metro: Moncloa
ⓘ Admission charge (free on Sun)

Museo Lázaro Galdiano

Shortly after the death of financier José Lázaro Galdiano (1862–1947), his neo-Renaissance house containing an extraordinary collection of 13,000 pieces of art was bequeathed to the nation. Eclectic is the only word to describe the displays, which range from a seventh-century BC Phoenician jug in which the spout is shaped like a cat's head to an assortment of paintings by, among others, Hieronymus Bosch, Van Eyck, El Greco, Goya, Constable, Gainsborough and Reynolds. 📍 Calle de Serrano 122 ☎ 915 61 60 84 🌐 www.flg.es 🕐 10.00–16.30 Wed–Mon, closed Aug Ⓜ Metro: Rubén Darío ⓘ Admission charge (free Sun)

Museo Sorolla

Spain's Impressionist painter Joaquin Sorolla is little known abroad but here in his former home and studio you can get to know his work, which is imbued with the bright Mediterranean sunlight of his native Valencia. There is also a collection of artworks by Sorolla's contemporaries and a garden designed by the artist. 📍 Paseo General Martínez Campos 37 ☎ 913 10 15 84 🌐 http://museosorolla.mcu.es
🕐 09.30–20.00 Tues–Sat, 10.00–15.00 Sun Ⓜ Metro: Iglesia
ⓘ Admission charge (free on Sun)

RETAIL THERAPY

Adolfo Dominguez Spanish designer known especially for his men's suits and shoes. 📍 José Ortega y Gasset 4 ☎ 915 77 82 80
🕐 10.00–20.30 Mon–Sat Ⓜ Metro: Nuñez de Balboa

Agatha Ruiz de la Prada The outlet of the Spanish designer whose clothes and accessories are characterised by colourful flowers and hearts. 🅐 Serrano 27 ☎ 913 19 05 01 🕐 10.00–14.00, 17.00–20.00 Mon–Fri Ⓜ Metro: Serrano

Amaya Arzuaga Hip, quasi-punky designs with a spectacular knitwear selection that is definitively not for grannies. Perfect for a special occasion. 🅐 Lagasca 50 ☎ 914 26 28 15 🕐 10.30–20.30 Mon–Sat Ⓜ Metro: Serrano or Velázquez

Bodegas Santa Cecilia Two shops are needed to stock the thousands of Spanish wines on sale. Regular taster sessions are held at No 72. 🅐 Blasco de Garay 72–74 ☎ 914 45 52 83 🕐 10.00–21.00 Mon–Sat Ⓜ Metro: Islas Filipinas

Camper Outpost of the internationally famous Mallorcan shoe company specialising in brightly coloured, soft leather shoes. Recently the rather child-like styles have been seriously sexed up. 🅐 Calle de Serrano 24 ☎ 915 78 25 60 🕐 10.00–20.30 Mon–Sat Ⓜ Metro: Serrano

Cuenllas A high-class delicatessen selling fine Spanish foods, including wines, cheeses, olive oils, pâtés and preserved bottled vegetables, plus imported foods (this is the best place in Madrid to buy English tea). 🅐 Ferraz 3 ☎ 915 47 31 33 🕐 09.00–14.00, 17.00–20.30 Mon–Sat, 09.00–14.30 Sun Ⓜ Metro: Plaza de España or Ventura Rodríguez

The Deli Room A fashion outlet selling ranges by a selection of Spanish designers. 🅐 Santa Barbara 4 (off Calle Fuencarral) ☎ 915 21 19 83 🕐 11.00–14.00, 17.00–21.00 Mon–Fri, 11.00–15.00, 17.00–21.00 Sat Ⓜ Metro: Tribunal or Gran Vía

🔺 *The flagship Madrid Camper shop charts the Spanish brand's history*

La Duquesita A family-run *pastelería* selling the delicious home-made cakes and sweets that have made it a Madrid institution.
🅐 Fernando VI 2 ☎ 913 08 02 31 🕐 09.30–14.30, 17.00–21.00 Tues–Sat, 17.00–21.00 Sun Ⓜ Metro: Alonso Martínez

Imaginarium Spain's most successful chain of toyshops is famous for its two-door entrance: one for the grown-ups and a tiny one for the kiddies. Inside, there's a huge range of carefully designed toys and games. 🅐 Claudio Coello 45 ☎ 917 81 33 37 🕐 10.00–21.00 Mon–Sat Ⓜ Metro: Serrano or Velázquez

Joaquín Berao A fashionable jewellery designer who specialises in solid silver jewellery at reasonably accessible prices.
ⓐ Claudio Coello 35 ⓣ 915 77 28 28 ⓛ 10.00–14.00, 17.00–20.30 Mon–Sat ⓝ Metro: Serrano

Lavinia If your interest in wine goes further than the corner shop's stock, you might want to poke your nose into what claims to be Europe's biggest wine shop, with 4,500 vintages to choose from and knowledgeable staff. ⓐ José Ortega y Gasset 16 ⓣ 914 26 05 99 ⓛ 10.00–21.00 Mon–Sat ⓝ Metro: Nuñez de Balboa

Lladró World-famous hand-made porcelain figurines from Valencia, prices ranging from hundreds of pounds to tens of thousands.
ⓐ Calle de Serrano 68 ⓣ 914 35 51 12 ⓛ 10.00–20.00 Mon–Sat ⓝ Metro: Serrano

Loewe There are standard bags and shoes and then there are Loewe bags and shoes. Come here for classic leather goods for men and women at prices reflecting their luxury. ⓐ Calle de Serrano 26 & 34 ⓣ 915 77 60 56 ⓛ 09.30–20.30 Mon–Sat ⓝ Metro: Serrano

Mango A Spanish fashion chain that's very popular with teenagers and young women. There's often a bargain section to rummage through. ⓐ Calle Fuencarral 70 ⓣ 915 23 04 12 ⓛ 10.00–21.00 Mon–Sat ⓝ Metro: Bilbao

Sybilla Upmarket women's fashion favoured by Spanish actresses and celebrities. The Jocomomola line is a little more affordable.
ⓐ Callejón de Jorge Juan 14 ⓣ 915 75 00 05 ⓛ 10.30–20.30 Mon–Sat ⓝ Metro: Retiro or Serrano

Up Beat Discos Stock up on retro music and fashion here. ⓐ Espíritu Santo 6 ⓣ 915 22 76 60 ⓛ 11.00–14.00, 17.00–20.30 Mon–Fri, 11.00–14.00 Sat ⓜ Metro: Tribunal or Noviciado

Walter Steiger The internationally famous women's shoe shop in the Salamanca district also sells handbags and a good range of men's footwear. ⓐ Lagasca 88 ⓣ 914 35 51 44 ⓛ 10.00–14.00, 16.30–20.00 Mon–Sat ⓜ Metro: Nuñez de Balboa or Rubén Darío

SHOPPING CENTRES

ABC Serrano An upmarket eight-floor shopping centre touting designer and high-street fashion, sportswear and jewellery. It also has restaurants and a gym. ⓐ Entrances at Calle de Serrano 61 & Paseo de la Castellana 64 ⓜ Metro: Rubén Darío, Nuñez de Balboa or Serrano

Azca You can't miss Azca as it's underneath the Torre Picasso skyscraper, halfway up the Paseo de la Castellana. It spreads between Paseo de la Castellana, Avenida del General Perón, Calle Orense and Calle Raimundo Fernández Villaverde – with entrances from all four streets. ⓜ Metro: Santiago Bernabeu or Nuevos Ministerios

El Jardin de Serrano A small, exclusive shopping centre where you'll find expensive designer clothes and shoes. ⓐ Calle de Goya 6, Salamanca ⓜ Metro: Serrano

TAKING A BREAK

El Bocaíto £ ❶ This place has been around forever and it looks like some of the bow-tied waiters have too. Come here for no-nonsense tapas surrounded by tiled walls and, naturally, plenty of bullfighting posters. Libertad 6 915 32 12 19 13.00–16.00, 20.30–24.00 Mon–Fri, 20.30–24.00 Sat Metro: Chueca

Stop Madrid £ ❷ This old charcuterie has retained many of its original 1920s fittings and remains one of the best stops for high-quality tapas in the area. You can order any of its 50 or so wines by the glass. Hortaleza 11 915 21 88 87 12.00–02.00 Metro: Chueca or Gran Vía

La Bardemcilla ££ ❸ A mecca for cinephiles, this stylish tapas bar and restaurant is owned by the Bardem family and is awash with film references. Augusto Figueroa 47 915 21 42 56 12.00–16.30, 20.00–02.30 Mon–Thur, 20.00–02.00 Fri & Sat Metro: Chueca

Hevia £££ ❹ One of the best of Madrid's new breed of smart and sophisticated tapas bars, Hevia serves up fancy little creations at splurge-level prices. Serrano 118 915 62 30 75 09.30–01.00 Mon–Sat Metro: Gregorio Marañón

AFTER DARK

RESTAURANTS

El Bierzo £ ❺ The combination of hearty, old-fashioned food, comfortable surroundings and irrepressibly jovial service keeps the locals coming back to this charming and very reasonably priced *casa de comidas*. Calle Barbieri 16 915 31 91 10 13.00–16.00, 20.00–23.30 Mon–Sat Metro: Chueca

tapas & raciones

	€
Pimientos Padrón	6,00
Pulpo a nosa feira	12,50
Croquetas Orixe	7,50
Tortilla jugosiña a Cacheiras	8,75
Tortilla Cambados	10,00
Tortilla Santiago	10,00
Tortilla Orixe	10,00
Empanada del dia	10,50
Choriziños al Albariño	6,00
Chorizos Criollos y Chimichurri	6,50
Albóndigas Ternera Orixe	10,00
Lacón cocido al estilo Lalín	7,00
Cecina de Ourense	9,00
Callos con garbanzos	10,50
Salteado Langostinos y Pulpo	13,50
Jamón Ibérico de Bellota	16,50
Tapas Calientes (unidad)	2,50
Tapas Frías (unidad)	2,20

▲ *Tapas are a must-do in Madrid*

Al-Jaima ££ ❻ Billed as 'desert cuisine', this excellent-value Middle Eastern restaurant packs in local diners on a budget. Low tables, incense and candlelight complement a great selection of tender tagines, dips, delectable felafel, honey-drenched baklava and mint tea. ⓐ Calle Barbieri 1 ❶ 915 23 11 42 ❷ 13.30–16.00, 21.30–24.00 ❼ Metro: Chueca or Gran Vía

La Dame Noire ££ ❼ The Moulin Rouge meets Catholic Spain in this unbeatably kitsch froth of Baroque cherubs and red velvet named after the black-clad virgin in the corner, who sternly presides over the plates of goat's cheese salad and chicken kebabs with raspberry coulis. ⓐ Pérez Galdós 3 (off Calle Fuencarral) ❶ 915 31 04 76 ❷ 21.00–24.00 Mon–Thur & Sun, 21.00–02.00 Fri & Sat ❼ Metro: Chueca or Tribunal

Teatriz ££ ❽ The stalls of the former theatre have been given a make-over by designer Philippe Starck and now make an unusual place to eat new-wave Italian cuisine. The toilets look as if they should be admired rather than used. ⓐ Calle Hermosilla 15 ❶ 915 77 53 79 ❷ 13.30–15.45, 21.00–23.00 ❼ Metro: Serrano

Thai Gardens ££ ❾ This was the first restaurant specialising in Thai cuisine to open in Spain. It has a peaceful atmosphere with its three dining rooms on three different levels, all prettily decorated with plants, Buddhas and subtle lighting. ⓐ Paseo de la Habana 3 ❶ 915 77 88 84 ❼ Metro: Nuevos Ministerios

Zalacaín £££ ❿ One of the best restaurants in Spain, if not Europe. Tip-top nosh for tip-top prices. ⓐ Calle Álvarez de Baena 4 ❶ 915 61 48 40 ❷ 13.15–16.00, 21.00–24.00, closed Sat lunch & all day Sun ❼ Metro: Gregorio Marañón

BARS

Binomio A beacon in gay Madrid, this ultra-camp cabaret club features magicians, flamenco drag queens and plenty of audience participation. ⓐ Corredera Baja de San Pablo 26 ❶ No phone Ⓜ Metro: Tribunal

Bodega de Angel Sierra A beautiful bar with frescoes on the ceiling and tiles on the walls. A popular place for lunch or an early evening drink in the sunny square. ⓐ Gravina 11, on Plaza de Chueca ❶ 915 31 01 26 Ⓜ Metro: Chueca

Castellana Ocho Hepcats dig the jazzy sounds in this impossibly smooth bar/restaurant/club with a popular street terrace. Don't miss Sunday brunch with live jazz. ⓐ Paseo de la Castellana 8 ❶ 915 78 34 87 Ⓜ Metro: Colón

LIVE MUSIC

Café la Palma Normally used by the locals as a *primera copa* bar – somewhere for a drink or two before going clubbing – although DJs and international live acts mean you can also dance here. ⓐ Calle de la Palma 62 ❶ 915 22 50 31 Ⓜ Metro: Noviciado ❶ Admission charge

Galileo Galilei The programme in this former cinema couldn't be more varied, including as it does dance and stand-up comedy. The music covers a broad spectrum from Latin to jazz, pop, folk, Celtic, a capella and flamenco-fusion, and there are occasional visits from big international names. ⓐ Calle Galileo 100 ❶ 915 34 75 57 Ⓜ Metro: Quevedo ❶ Admission charge

Sala Clamores A long-running and well-reputed jazz club serving excellent cocktails. Although the aim is to re-create a jazz dive in the American tradition, many of the acts come from other musical roots: blues, gospel, folk and even pop, tango and funk. Calle Alburquerque 14 (Chamberí) 914 45 79 38 www.salaclamores.com Metro: Bilbao Admission charge

CLUBS

Areia Billed as a 'colonial chillout' serving cocktails. The DJs play a variety of dance music, including 'eclectic bizarre', minimal, chill house, dub and funk. Calle de Hortaleza 92 913 10 03 07 www.areiachillout.com Metro: Chueca

Moma56 A stylish bar and restaurant complex with resident and visiting DJs, and live shows from Wednesday to Sunday. Calle de José Abascal 56 (right next to Plaza Doctor Marañón) 913 99 09 00 Metro: Gregorio Marañón Admission charge

Pacha Don't expect anything like the Ibiza mothership, but for a taste of Balearic glam this Madrid outpost is great. Dress up and suck in those cheekbones to get past the bouncers. Barceló 11 914 47 01 28 Metro: Tribunal Admission charge

Tula A generation of *madrileños* has grown up with this *bar de copas*, which opened in the 1980s at the height of the 'La Movida' years. Its agreeable 1960s atmosphere has guaranteed its popularity since. Claudio Coello 116 914 27 60 43 www.bartula.es Metro: Gregorio Marañón

The royal fortress at Segovia, the Alcázar

 OUT OF TOWN
trips

Around Madrid

Day-trippers are spoilt for choice in Madrid, which lies right in the centre of a ring of interesting towns and historic sights. The city is also well connected by radiating motorways and the wonderfully efficient *cercanías* railway system that can whisk you quickly beyond the suburbs.

All the places in this section are close enough to visit on a day out, but we've recommended hotels if you want to make a night of it. Most places are accessible by public transport, but if you want to get a true flavour of rural Spain, a car is essential.

If you have limited time, the obvious place to head for is the royal palace-monastery of El Escorial, which you can combine with a trip to the nearby Valle de los Caídos war memorial. With more time, you might want to explore lesser-known places within reach of Madrid such as Chinchón, Guadalajara and Alcalá de Henares.

Alternatively, if you want to get right out of town, you could make for the Sierra de Guadarrama, which forms a protective barrier across Madrid's northern back, or the Sierra de Gredos, a little further away to the west.

ALCALÁ DE HENARES

At first glance this satellite town doesn't look like a World Heritage Site – but at its heart is the dignified remnant of a university that was famed for its learning in 16th-century Europe, particularly in the field of languages. Alcalá was the world's first planned university city and was intended to serve as a *Civitas Dei* ('City of God'), an ideal urban community to be used as a model when founding towns in the Americas. The oldest surviving part of the university,

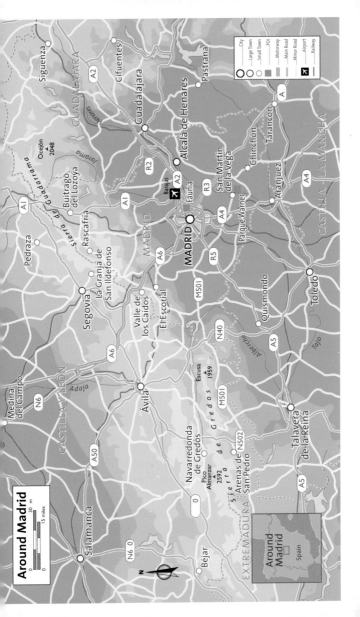

the Colegio de San Ildefonso, has a plateresque façade and several handsome patios. Alcalá was also the birthplace of Catherine of Aragón (1485–1536), Henry VIII's first wife, and of Miguel de Cervantes, the author of *Don Quixote*, born here in 1547 (the exact date is not known). The house where he was born is open to the public.

GETTING THERE

Take the Cercanías C-2 or C-7a train; they run about every 10 minutes. From Alcalá de Henares Station, it's about a 10-minute walk down the Paseo de la Estación into the city centre.

Alternatively, take an Alsa bus (❶ 902 42 22 42) number 223 from Avenida de America metro station. They leave roughly every 10 minutes.

RETAIL THERAPY

Convento de San Diego A convent in which Franciscan nuns make and sell traditional *almendras garrapiñadas*, sugar-coated almonds. ❷ Calle Beatas 7 ❶ 918 88 03 05

TAKING A BREAK

There are several places in Alcalá de Henares where you can eat tapas. Some of the best are **Barataria** (❷ Cerrajeros 18), **La Casa Vieja** (❷ San Felipe Neri 3) and **El Pollo de Alcalá** (❷ Vía Complutense 32).

Alcaravea ££ A no-frills *cervecería* (bar specialising in beers) that serves excellent tapas and pinchos, both hot and cold. At lunchtime there is a good-value *menú del día*. ❷ Avenida Juan Carlos I 13 ❶ 918 30 54 30

CHINCHÓN

The old town of Chinchón is picturesquely gathered around a charming 16th-century galleried plaza, which is used at different times of year as a venue for a bullfight (August) and for the staging of an Easter Week passion play. You can get a view of the town from the castle that stands above it. ⓦ www.ciudad-chinchon.com

🔺 *The quiet cloisters of Alcalá University*

GETTING THERE

Take bus 337 (La Veloz) from Conde de Casal metro station (1 hour).

RETAIL THERAPY

Chinchón is renowned for its anís, a spirit flavoured with aniseed, and you can buy bottles in the main square. The town is also known for its garlic.

◗ *The Plaza Mayor in Chinchón offers food and accommodation in historic surrounds*

TAKING A BREAK

Most of the restaurants offer the typical Chinchón fare of garlic soup followed by roast lamb and suckling pig.

Mesón de la Virreina ££ A 16th-century building with a traditional *balconada* (balcony) on the town's main square, serving real Castilian food such as roast suckling pig and *sopa castellana* – a reinvigorating thick garlic soup. It also serves local wines.
ⓐ Plaza Mayor 28 ⓣ 918 94 00 15 ⓦ www.mesonvirreyna.com

ACCOMMODATION

Parador de Chinchón £££ A converted 17th-century monastery belonging to the state-owned network of Parador hotels. Built around a courtyard, it is full of antiques, frescoes and other pretty details. ⓐ Calle de los Huertos 1 ⓣ 918 94 08 36 ⓦ www.parador.es

EL ESCORIAL

Everybody's number one day trip from Madrid has to be to this massive palace-monastery. King Felipe II had it built by architect Juan de Herrera when the Spanish empire was at the height of its power and wealth. In size and scope, it is truly daunting, although the austere and sober outside is at odds with the fineries within. You could do El Escorial in a morning or afternoon, but if you have the time, give yourself the best part of a day to get here and enjoy it.

🔺 *El Escorial is a perfect day trip from Madrid*

FAUNIA

This pioneering project aimed mainly at children is both fun and educational. It calls itself a 'nature theme park' but is really an animated, up-to-date natural history museum-cum-zoo divided into ecosystems that are inhabited by 200 species of animals. ❸ Avenida de las Comunidades 28 ☎ 913 01 62 10 ⓦ www.faunia.es ⏱ Timetables change every month Ⓝ Metro: Valdebernardo ⓘ Admission charge

There are four parts to the complex: the monastery, the church (which you can see without buying a ticket), the library with its magnificently decorated vaulted ceiling (whose holdings are said to rival those of the Vatican), and the Friars' garden – a good place to stroll when you need to get your breath back.

To see everything you can either join a guided tour (which takes about 45 minutes) or follow the signs around yourself, in which case you'll need up to 2 hours. You shouldn't get lost as the building is laid out on a grid pattern that is supposed to symbolise the martyrdom of St Lawrence (San Lorenzo), who was roasted alive on a gridiron and to whom El Escorial is dedicated.

As well as the library, don't miss: the understated Royal Apartments, which reflect the diminutive Felipe's nature as part-monk part-frugal bureaucrat; the Royal Pantheon, where the remains of most of Spain's monarchs lie in black marble sarcophagi (the tiny, wedding-cake-style infant pantheon is particularly moving); and the church with the statues of Felipe II and three of his wives kneeling in prayer (Mary Tudor, whom he never liked, is conspicuously absent). It is essential to book the guided tour at least one day in advance.

VALLE DE LOS CAÍDOS

Having inflicted a decisive and humiliating victory on government forces in the Spanish Civil War, Franco wasn't going to let the affair be forgotten. In the early years of the peace he had thousands of prisoners of war hack a colossal subterranean church out of the foothills of the Guadarrama Mountains and surmount it with a towering concrete cross. The whole thing is supposed to be a war memorial in the neutral sense of the word with soldiers of both sides buried here, but Franco reserved pride of place for his own tomb, along with that of José Antonio Primo de Rivera, founder of the Falange (Fascist) party. Inevitably, the political symbolism of the 'Valley of the Fallen' divides opinion but it is still an awesome monument and a fascinating example of the vanity and folly of dictatorship in stark contrast to the tolerance of modern Spain. If nothing else, the natural setting among pinewoods is very attractive and there are great views from the cross, which is reached by a footpath. ⓐ 13 km (8 miles) north of El Escorial by small roads; pay at the entrance gate before continuing 6 km (4 miles) through the woods to the main car park ⓣ 918 90 56 11 ⓦ www.patrimonionacional.es ⓛ 10.00–18.30 Tues–Sun (Apr–Sept); 10.00–17.30 Tues–Sun (Oct–Mar) ⓝ Bus: 660 (Autocares Herranz) from San Lorenzo de El Escorial (10 minutes). ⓘ Admission charge

ⓐ San Lorenzo de El Escorial, on Autovía A6 towards La Coruña ⓣ 918 90 59 03 ⓦ www.patrimonionacional.es ⓛ 10.00–17.00 Tues–Sun (Oct–Mar); 10.00–18.00 Tues–Sun (Apr–Sept). Closed public holidays ⓘ Admission charge

● *Franco's folly – the* Valle de los Caídos

GETTING THERE

Take bus 664 or 661 (Autocares Herranz) from Moncloa metro station (about an hour). Or take the train (line C-8) from Atocha Station (50 minutes plus 2 km (1-mile) walk).

TAKING A BREAK

Parilla Príncipe ££ This intimate 18th-century palace has rooms on the upper floors and a lovely peaceful restaurant below serving an interesting combination of fine seafood and hefty Castilian classics such as roast lamb. ❷ Floridablanca 6, San Lorenzo de El Escorial ❶ 918 90 16 11 ⓦ www.parrillaprincipe.com ❶ Closed Tues

ACCOMMODATION

El Botánico £££ An exquisitely renovated 18th-century stone palace with a beautiful garden and good views of El Escorial. All its bedrooms are individually styled. It also boasts an excellent restaurant.
🅰 Timoteo Padrós 16, San Lorenzo de El Escorial ☎ 918 90 78 79
🅦 www.labuganvilla.es

SIERRA DE GREDOS

These mountains to the west of Madrid are a popular place to escape for a scenic drive or a weekend's hiking. To catch their flavour, take the N502 that crosses the range from the A5 (Madrid to Extremadura) motorway towards Ávila by means of the Puerto del Pico, a 1,352 m (4,435 ft) pass. On the way up the steep southern slopes that climb to the pass the road crosses and recrosses a dramatically zigzagging restored Roman road. Lower down, in a field near San Martín de Valdeiglesias, are four roughly carved granite figures of bulls, the Toros de Guisando, whose age and purpose are unknown.

GETTING THERE

There are buses from Madrid (Estación Sur) and from Ávila to Arenas de San Pedro, the main town of the Sierra de Gredos. If you're driving, take the R5, then the A5 from Madrid towards Extremadura and turn off at Talavera de la Reina on to the N502.

ACCOMMODATION

La Casa de Arriba ££ A cosy place with great mountain views suitable for chilling out or using as a base for hiking. 🅰 La Cruz 19, Navarredonda de Gredos ☎ 920 34 80 24 🅦 www.casadearriba.com

PARQUE WARNER

About as far from typical Spain as you could get without leaving the country, this theme park is a refreshing place to head if you've had enough of palaces and museums. The world of Hollywood is divided into five sections comprising 25 rides and other attractions: Old West Territory (on the theme of the Wild West), DC Superheroes, Hollywood Boulevard (with replicas of famous streets and sets including Bogart's Casablanca bar), Cartoon Village and Warner Brothers Studios. ⓐ San Martín de la Vega, A4 to Andalucia, exit at Km 22 ⓣ 902 02 41 00 ⓦ www.parquewarner.com ⓛ Apr–Oct (opening hours vary so check the website for details) ⓝ Train: C-3 from Atocha Station, there is a stop inside the park ⓘ Admission charge

Parador de Gredos £££ This stone building high in the beautiful Sierra de Gredos was the first hotel of the state-owned Parador network. It has wonderful views and is an ideal base for walking in the mountains. ⓐ Carretera Barranco-Béjar Km 42, Navarredonda de Gredos ⓣ 920 34 80 48 ⓦ www.parador.es

SIERRA DE GUADARRAMA

The Sierra de Guadarrama forms a solid barrier of mountains across Madrid's northern back, reaching to 2,430 m (7,970 ft) at the summit of Peñalara. In winter *madrileños* flock to ski resorts such as Puerto de Navacerrada, but for the rest of the year Guadarrama's pine-clad slopes are visited only by hikers.

At the foot of the mountains, at Rascafría, is the Monasterio de Santa María de El Paular, a monastery founded in 1390 and now also a hotel. Between Rascafría and Madrid is the handsome 15th-century **Castillo de Manzanares El Real** (☎ 918 53 00 08 ⏰ 10.00–17.00 Tues–Fri, 10.00–19.00 Sat & Sun, last entry 1 hour before closing time ❶ Admission charge).

Towards the northeastern end of the mountains is the tranquil walled town of Buitrago del Lozoya, which has an Arab *alcázar* (castle) and a church with a pretty Mudéjar tower.

GETTING THERE

Trains from Atocha and Chamartín stations run into the sierra at Ceredilla (line C-8b). From there, a connecting line (C-9) stops at a string of small stations, including Puerto de Navacerrada, before terminating in Cotos.

ACCOMMODATION

Santa María del Paular £££ A luxury hotel in part of a Benedictine monastery beneath the Sierra de Guadarrama. It also has a restaurant as well as a more informal *mesón*. ❸ Carretera Monasterio del Paular, Rascafría ☎ 918 69 10 11 ⓦ www.sheratonpaular.com

GUADALAJARA & SIGÜENZA

The only thing to see in the small provincial city of Guadalajara is the magnificent Palacio de los Duques del Infantado, which dates mainly from the 15th century. If you're passing, it's certainly worth driving into town to admire its florid Gothic Mudéjar façade. Further from Madrid is the smaller but much more rewarding town of Sigüenza, which is dominated by its castle, now a Parador hotel. The cathedral contains *El Doncel*, a sculpture of a young nobleman reclining on a tombstone and reading his way through eternity.

GETTING THERE

For Guadalajara, Cercanías C1 and C2 trains leave Atocha or Chamartín stations every half hour and the journey takes 1 hour. For Sigüenza, take lines to Zaragoza, leaving frequently from any RENFE station (such as Atocha or Chamartín).

Samar (☎ 902 25 70 25 ⓦ www.samar.es) runs bus services from Madrid Estación Sur to Guadalajara. The journey takes 45 minutes to an hour.

If you'd rather take the car to Guadalajara, take exit 55 from the A2 Madrid–Barcelona road. For Sigüenza, take the A2 turning off at Km 103 and take the CM1101 to the town itself.

⬥ *The rolling landscape around Sigüenza*

Cities of Old Castile

The three historic cities of Ávila, Segovia and Salamanca lie beyond the Sierra de Guadarrama and the Sierra de Gredos in the vast territory of Castilla y León. All are within easy reach of Madrid and at a pinch could be visited in a day trip – certainly the closest of them, Segovia, is only a short hop from Madrid. They do, however, merit a more leisurely visit and can easily be combined in a short tour. Allow the most time for the handsome and lively university city of Salamanca. (See map on page 107.)

GETTING THERE

RENFE trains depart from Atocha and Chamartín stations every 2 hours or so for Salamanca (passing Ávila on the way) and Segovia. Direct trains take 1 hour 30 minutes to Ávila and Segovia and 2 hours to Salamanca.

Regular buses from Madrid's Estación Sur to Ávila and Salamanca are run by Avanzabus (📞 902 02 00 52 🌐 www.avanzabus.com). To Segovia, La Sepulvedana (📞 902 11 96 99 🌐 www.lasepulvedana.es) leaves from Paseo de la Florida.

ÁVILA

Ávila was the birthplace of St Teresa, who lived an indefatigable life of high achievement between 1515 and 1582. She founded 15 convents for her order, the Carmelitas Descalzas (barefoot Carmelite nuns), and 17 more indirectly. She is also considered one of the finest writers Spain has produced and more mundanely gave her name to *yemas de Santa Teresa*, a sweet delicacy of candied egg yolks on sale absolutely everywhere in modern Ávila. The main attraction here is the city's perfect ring of walls.

● *Ávila's remarkable medieval city walls*

Tourist information ⓐ San Segundo 17 ⓣ 920 21 13 87
ⓦ www.turismocastillayleon.com

SIGHTS & ATTRACTIONS

The main reason for making the trek to the highest provincial capital
city in Europe at 1,131 m (3,710 ft) is to see the magnificent medieval
walls that encircle it. They stretch for about 2 km (1¼ miles) and there
are 88 towers and 9 gateways spaced out along them. For the best
view of the famous walls, cross the River Adaja to Los Cuatro Postes,
a small monument with four Doric columns.

The cathedral forms part of the walls. The nave is Gothic and there
are two pulpits of decorative wrought iron. A 15th-century cardinal,
Alonso de Madrigal, who was nicknamed *El Tostado* ('the Swarthy')
because of his dark complexion, is buried here. Outside the walls, the
Romanesque church of San Vicente is also worth seeing, mainly for
its carved west portal.

RETAIL THERAPY

La Bodeguita de San Segundo This typical *taberna* sells 500 kinds of wine. It is also a good-value place to eat. ⓐ San Segundo 19 ⓣ 920 25 73 09

La Flor de Castilla Established in 1860, this delicatessen sells excellent cakes and the typical sweets of Ávila, *yemas de Santa Teresa*. ⓐ Plaza de José Tomé 4 ⓣ 920 21 11 58

TAKING A BREAK

Mesón del Rastro ££ This lovely tavern matches the mounted boars' heads and roaring log fires with traditional Ávilan cuisine: try the *chuletónes de Ávila* – large steaks from the Iberian black fighting bull – served with locally grown beans. ⓐ Plaza del Rastro 1 ⓣ 920 21 12 19 ⓛ Closed for dinner on Mon, Tues & Wed

El Molino de la Losa ££ In a pretty setting next to the river, this restaurant in an old flour mill serves lamb, suckling pig and steaks (*chuletónes de Ávila*). ⓐ Bajada de la Losa 12 ⓣ 920 21 11 02 ⓛ Closed Mon

El Almacén £££ From the big windows of this old converted warehouse there are views of the city's walls. The cuisine is imaginative and the wine list excellent. ⓐ Carretera de Salamanca 6 ⓣ 920 21 10 26 ⓛ Closed Sun evening, Mon & Sept

ACCOMMODATION

Hospedería La Sinagoga ££ A beautifully restored 15th-century synagogue in the pedestrianised part of the city, located between the cathedral and the town hall. ⓐ Reyes Católicos 22 ⓣ 920 35 23 21

Parador de Turismo de Ávila £££ A renovated 16th-century mansion forming part of the state-run Parador network of historic hotels.
ⓐ Marqués de Canales de Chozas 2 ❶ 920 21 13 40 ⓦ www.parador.es

SALAMANCA

This magnificent university city is a joy to stroll around, with handsome buildings of golden sandstone almost everywhere you look. What could have been a clash of styles – Gothic, Renaissance, plateresque and Baroque – has grown over the centuries into a pleasing whole. As well as the sights listed below look out for the *Casa de las Muertes* (House of the Dead) on Calle Bordadores with a skull carved into its façade, and

SALAMANCA'S TWIN CATHEDRALS

Behind the university are Salamanca's two cathedrals, the old and the new. Despite being in very different architectural styles, they work well together. You have to go through the new one, **Catedral Nueva** (ⓐ Plaza Anaya 🕐 09.00–20.00), to get to the older, Romanesque **Catedral Vieja** (ⓐ Plaza Anaya 🕐 10.00–19.30 ❶ Admission charge except 10.00–12.00 Tues) which has a huge altarpiece made of 53 painted panels by Nicolás Florentino. Commissioned by Ferdinand II, the 'new' cathedral dates mainly from the 16th century with a few elements from the 18th century. Its intricately carved Gothic west front is impressive, but entering through the north façade of the 'new' cathedral (off Plaza de Anaya) also note the tiny stone carvings around the central archway, including bulls, rabbits, pigs and even an astronaut, added during renovations.

two towers, the Torre del Clavero and the Torre del Aire, which remain adrift from the vanished mansions to which they once belonged.

Tourist information ⓐ Plaza Mayor 14 ⓣ 923 21 83 42
ⓦ www.salamanca.es

SIGHTS & ATTRACTIONS

Casa de las Conchas

The Rúa Mayor, leading south from the Plaza Mayor, takes you directly to this 16th-century mansion named after the 400 scallop shells carved on its walls. ⓐ Calle Compañia 2 ⓛ 09.00–21.00 Mon–Fri; 09.00–14.00, 16.00–19.00 Sat; 10.00–14.00, 16.00–19.00 Sun

Convento de las Dueñas

Admire the Renaissance patio on two floors. ⓐ Plaza Concilio de Trento ⓛ 11.30–12.45, 16.30–17.30 (Oct–Mar); 10.30–12.45, 16.30–18.45 (Apr–Sept) ⓘ Admission charge

Plaza Mayor

The Plaza Mayor, one of the largest and finest public spaces in Spain, was laid out with Baroque grandeur in the 18th century. Two distinctive buildings stare at each other across it: the Ayuntamiento (city hall) and the Royal Pavilion. There are inviting cafés in the arcades of the other buildings around the square.

University

From the Patio de las Escuelas, you can admire the chiselled detail of the university's plateresque façade. A carved medallion portrays Fernando and Isabel, the 'Catholic Monarchs', who unified Spain in 1492 and dispatched Columbus to discover the New World. A gateway off the Patio de las Escuelas leads into the charming Patio de las Escuelas

▲ *The Patio de las Escuelas Menores in Salamanca*

Menores. ② Patio de las Escuelas 🕐 09.30–13.00, 16.00–19.00
Mon–Sat, 10.00–13.00 Sun ⓘ Admission charge

RETAIL THERAPY

Artempera This art studio specialises in quality reproductions of
paintings and other masterworks. It supplies museums, hotels and
private collectors. ② Calle Valencia 20, Oficina 191

La Tahona A bakery and delicatessen in the centre of Salamanca,
selling cakes, quality preserves and a good seleciton of wines. ② Paseo
Carmelitas 23 ⓘ 923 26 61 35

🔺 *The Plaza Mayor in Salamanca*

TAKING A BREAK

Plaza Mayor You can't do better than taking an outdoor table in one of the cafés in the Plaza Mayor, although you'll pay for the privilege. There are cheaper places to eat in the Plaza del Mercado and around the university.

Restaurante Cordovilla ££ Located a short walk from the Plaza Mayor, this restaurant specialises in traditional Castilian cuisine, including *cocidos* and *embutidos* (sausages), but also does fish and vegetable dishes. 🄰 Condes de Crespo Rascon 11 🕿 923 21 39 62

Chez Víctor £££ French and Spanish food, including superb desserts. Try the crab and apple salad, and the chocolate and peanut toffee. 🄰 Espoz y Mina 26 🕿 923 21 31 23 🕒 Closed Sun evening, Mon & Aug

Río de la Plata £££ Had enough suckling pig? You can order excellent fish in this typical *mesón* next to the Plaza Mayor. It's small, popular and busy. ❸ Plaza del Peso 1 ❶ 923 21 90 05 ❻ Closed Mon & July

AFTER DARK

Salamanca is a very studenty city and the nightlife is good in term time, at the weekends and in the summer. The three main areas are on and around the Gran Vía (try **El Callejon**, **Versus**, **Atenea**, **El Savor** and **Bakudo**); in Bordadores (**Morgana**, **Caché**, **Niebla** and **Camelot**); and around the Plaza Mayor (**Belle Epoque**, **Cum Laude** and **Bolero**).

ACCOMMODATION

Condal ££ This modern and functional hotel in the centre is conveniently situated for visiting the Old Town. It has special offers for weekend stays. ❸ Plaza Santa Eulalia 3–5 ❶ 923 21 84 00 ❿ www.hotelcondal.com

San Polo ££ Located very close to the cathedrals, with great bedrooms and one suite with a wonderful view. No parking. ❸ Arroyo de Santo Domingo 2–4 ❶ 923 21 11 77 ❿ www.hotelsanpolo.com

Rector £££ Situated at the entrance of the monumental part of the city, this hotel hides behind a rather modest façade. Inside, the bedrooms are spacious and comfortable. ❸ Paseo del Rector Esparabé 10 ❶ 923 21 84 82 ❿ www.hotelrector.com

SEGOVIA

SIGHTS & ATTRACTIONS

Two prominent but very different monuments make Segovia a must-visit destination. One is its fairy-tale royal fortress, the Alcázar, and the other is the Roman aqueduct. In between these two sights is the Old Town, built around the **Plaza Mayor** and the **cathedral**. More interesting, however, are Segovia's Romanesque churches, notably the 11th-century **San Juan de los Caballeros** and, outside the Old Town, the 13th-century **Vera Cruz**, which owes its origins to the Knights Templar.

When it's time for lunch, Segovia's speciality is *cochinillo asado*, wood-fire roasted suckling pig; nearly every restaurant window portrays an unfortunate porker with an apple in its mouth.
Tourist information ⓐ Plaza Mayor 10 ⓣ 921 46 60 70
ⓦ www.segoviaturismo.es

Alcázar

This soars above an outcrop of rock with the perfect turrets of a Disneyland castle. Its earliest parts are from the 12th century but what you see today owes more to a programme of rebuilding after a fire in 1862. Inside are ornate chambers, including the Throne Room, the Galley Room (so named because before the fire it was reminiscent of an upturned ship), the King's Chamber and the Monarchs' Room. Before you leave don't forget to climb the Torre de Juan II for a view over Segovia. ⓛ 10.00–19.00 (Apr–Sept); 10.00–18.00 (Oct–Mar) ⓘ Admission charge

Roman aqueduct

The city's other unmistakable structure is the aqueduct that still strides nonchalantly over the Plaza Azoguejo in a series of ingeniously

⬥ *The cathedral at Segovia*

⬥ *The spires of the Alcázar, Segovia*

simple double arches. At its highest it is 95 m (312 ft) tall. It was in
almost continual use from the 1st century until the 19th century.

La Granja de San Ildefonso

There is a strong whiff of the French King Louis XIV's palace of Versailles
in this Spanish Bourbon pleasure-dome outside Segovia, which grew
out of a hunting lodge under the auspices of Felipe V in the 18th
century. Fire damaged many of the rooms in 1918, but you probably
won't be able to tell the difference between original and restoration
as you take the guided tour through ornate chamber after ornate
chamber. Particularly worth seeing are the large chandeliers made in
Spain's royal glass factory. If the palace is not for you then you may still
enjoy the landscaped gardens, with their fountains, chestnut woods
and maze. ⓐ 11 km (7 miles) southeast of Segovia ⓣ 921 47 00 19

🕐 10.00–13.30, 15.00–17.00 Tues–Sat, 10.00–14.00 Sun (Oct–Mar); 10.00–18.00 Tues–Sun (Apr–Sept) ❶ Admission charge

RETAIL THERAPY

Supreme (❷ Cronista Lecea 11) is a delicatessen selling local specialities, while **Monjas Dominicas** (❷ Calle Capuchinas Altas 2) stocks a selection of the best local crafts.

TAKING A BREAK

The tourist drag up Calle Juan Bravo is lined with overpriced eateries, so try to avoid them if possible.

Duque ££ Opened in 1895, this family-owned restaurant is one of the city's favourite eateries. It's a good place to order *cochinillo asado* (suckling pig) or lamb. Reservations are recommended at weekends. ❷ Cervantes 12 ❶ 921 46 24 87

Mesón de Cándido £££ Ask for a table with a view of Segovia's famous aqueduct in this restaurant serving suckling pig. ❷ Plaza del Azoguejo 5 ❶ 921 42 59 11 ❿ www.mesondecandido.es

ACCOMMODATION

Caserío de Lobones £££ An elegant old farmhouse situated in peaceful countryside, not far outside the city of Segovia. ❷ Valverde del Majano ❶ 921 12 84 08 ❿ www.lobones.com

Infanta Isabel £££ Located in the city's main square, this modern hotel in a renovated 19th-century building has comfortable and well-equipped bedrooms. ❷ Plaza Mayor ❶ 921 46 13 00 ❿ www.hotelinfantaisabel.com

Toledo & La Mancha

Travel south from Madrid and you cross the Iberian peninsula's longest river, the Tajo (or Tagus), to emerge on the plains of La Mancha, famed as the haunt of Don Quixote and important today for the wine industry and its ubiquitous namesake cheese of Manchego, the cheddar of Spain. La Mancha has a few worthwhile sights to see but you have to drive dusty distances to find them.

GETTING THERE

High-speed AVE trains leave Atocha Station regularly for Toledo, taking 25 minutes to cover the distance. However, it's a long walk from the train station to the historical part of Toledo. **Alsa-Continental** (❶ 902 42 22 42 Ⓦ www.alsa.es) buses depart for Toledo from Estación Plaza Elíptica on Avenida Lusitania (on Metro lines 6 and 11) around every half an hour, taking about 50 minutes for the journey.

To explore the rest of La Mancha and villages like Puerto Lápice, El Toboso, Consuegra and Campo de Criptana, there are no nearby trains and only patchy bus services. As you are likely to want to hop fairly quickly from one village to the next, a hire car is by far the best option.

TOLEDO

SIGHTS & ATTRACTIONS
Before Madrid became the capital in 1561, Toledo was the most important city in Spain, being the seat of the Primate of Spain and home of the imperial court. Perched high on a hill and surrounded on three sides by the River Tagus, Toledo is a natural fortress and has held a vital position ever since Roman civilisation finally crumbled in the

🔺 *Toledo has a long and fascinating history*

Iberian peninsula in the sixth century. It was in Toledo that the Visigoths established their capital before being eclipsed in turn by invading Muslims from North Africa. Toledo, however, continued to be an important city throughout the Middle Ages and it was distinguished by a pluralist society in which Muslims, Jews and Christians not only coexisted amicably but culturally inspired each other. Known as the City of Three Cultures, Toledo became a famous seat of learning, founding schools of theology, mysticism, mathematics and astrology.

The centre of the city is an agreeable tangle of steep, narrow streets creeping over a mound that is bordered in three directions by a sweeping curve of the River Tagus, and guarded on the fourth side by a wall. There are good viewpoints on the ring road on the

other side of the river but the best place to see the city in its entirety is from the terrace of the Parador (see Accommodation on page 138).

Few synagogues survive in Spain and the two fine examples in Toledo are but a faint reflection of the thriving Jewish community that once lived here.

Tourist information ⓐ Puerta de Bisagra ⓣ 925 22 08 43
ⓦ www.toledo.es

Alcázar

From wherever you look at it, the skyline of Toledo is dominated by the Alcázar, a 16th-century palace-fortress that was famously besieged during the Civil War. A legend – well known in Spain and repeated to every visitor to the Alcázar – tells how the leader of the Nationalists, Colonel Moscardó, was telephoned by a Republican officer and told that his son was being held hostage and would be killed if the garrison did not capitulate. Moscardó is supposed to have told his son over the phone, without hesitation: 'Shout Viva España and die like a hero.' The fate of the boy is unclear, but the Alcázar survived the siege and handed Franco a great propaganda victory. The Alcázar is soon to reopen as the country's premier military museum; the holdings of Madrid's Museo del Ejército are currently being catalogued and moved to the new site. ⓐ Cuesta de Carlos V ⓣ 925 22 16 73 ⓛ Closed for refurbishment

Cathedral

Toledo's absolutely jaw-dropping Gothic cathedral took over 250 years to build and mixes several styles. It is probably the richest of Spain's many cathedrals, as befits holy Toledo, the ecclesiastical heart of the country: features of particular interest include the carvings in the choir depicting the fall of the city of Granada to a Christian army, a colourful reredos behind the altar and Narcisco Tomé's utterly original Transparente, a Baroque altarpiece lit up by a skylight decorated with alabaster angels and pudgy putti. The chapterhouse, meanwhile, has a Mudéjar ceiling and the treasury contains an enormous 16th-century silver monstrance, which is carried through the streets during Corpus Christi processions. The sacristy houses paintings by El Greco, Titian, Van Dyck and Goya. ⓐ Plaza del Ayuntamiento ① 925 22 22 41 ⓛ 10.00–18.30 Mon–Sat, 16.00–18.30 Sun ① Admission charge

Santa María la Blanca

Though converted into a church, Santa María la Blanca retains a strange confluence of the three prevailing religions of the Golden Age of Toledo: stars of David carved in stone blend with the horseshoe arches typical of Islamic mosques and a gaudy Catholic altar. ⓐ Reyes Católicos 2 ① 925 22 72 57 ⓛ 10.00–18.45 (Apr–Sept); 10.00–17.45 (Oct–Mar) ① Admission charge

Singagoga del Tránsito

It looks uninteresting from the outside but inside has magnificent Mudéjar decoration. Part of it is a museum. ⓐ Samuel Leví ① 925 22 36 65 ⓛ 10.00–18.00 Tues–Sat (winter); 10.00–21.00 Tues–Sat, 10.00–14.00 Sun (summer) ① Admission charge

RETAIL THERAPY

Several shops have been selling blue and yellow ceramics made in nearby Talavera de la Reina since the 15th century, but the city's best-known craft is damascene work – black steel inlaid with gold, silver and copper wire. Ornamental damascene swords and jewellery are popular souvenirs. Those who are sweet of tooth should try Toledo's sweet almond marzipan.

EL GRECO

For 30 years Domenikos Theotokopoulos, universally known as El Greco because of his Greek origins, lived and worked in the city of Toledo. Although not born Spanish, he is regarded as one of the country's finest painters.

You can see his sometimes eerie paintings (for a time people weren't sure whether he was mentally ill) in many places in Toledo, not least in the **Museo de El Greco** (🄰 Calle Samuel Leví 3 🄸 925 22 44 05 🄲 Closed for refurbishment), which is dedicated to his memory. The **Museo de Santa Cruz** (🄰 Cervantes 3 🄸 925 22 10 36 🄲 10.00–18.30 Mon–Sat, 10.00–14.00 Sun) has 18 of his paintings displayed on the first floor along with other masterpieces from the 16th and 17th centuries. His best-known work, *The Burial of the Count of Orgaz*, still hangs on the arched wall of the church for which it was originally painted, the **Iglesia de Santo Tomé** (🄰 Plaza del Conde 1 🄸 925 25 60 98 🄲 10.00–18.45 (summer); 10.00–17.45 (winter) 🄸 Admission charge). The two figures looking out of the painting towards the viewer are thought to be El Greco's son, Jorge (bottom left), and, among the ruffed bystanders and looking directly at the viewer, El Greco himself.

TAKING A BREAK

Plaza de Zocodover is the liveliest square in which to hang out, with plenty of bars and restaurants, although things are cheaper if you wander a little off the beaten track. The terrace bars dotted around the Corral de Don Diego are particularly attractive.

Asador Adolfo ££ Toledo's justly famed eatery specialises in the local dish of slow-roasted stuffed partridge but also serves lighter, more modern dishes, complemented by an exhaustive wine list. ❷ Granada 6 ❶ 925 22 73 21 ❸ Closed Sun evening

Los Cuatro Tiempos ££ When you tire of partridge, this luxurious restaurant in a 16th-century mansion serves up stylish and sophisticated cuisine with locally sourced ingredients and excellent wines. ❷ Sixto Ramón Parro 5 ❶ 925 22 37 82 ❸ Closed Sun evening

Venta de Aires ££ This venerable restaurant near the Tajo River and city walls has been serving meat, fish and game since 1891. There's a good house menu (*menú de la casa*). ❷ Circo Romano 35 ❶ 925 22 05 45 ❿ www.ventadeaires.com

ACCOMMODATION

La Almazara £ This is an unusual, comfortable and welcoming place to stay if you don't mind being well outside the city across the River Tagus. The hotel stands amid juniper, olive and ilex trees in a spot that often drew El Greco in search of inspiration. Nine of the rooms have their own terraces with views of Toledo. ❷ Carretera Toledo-Cuerba Km 3.4 ❶ 925 22 38 66 ❿ www.hotelalmazara.com

Pintor El Greco £–££ A refurbished 17th-century bakery that has preserved its original façade and inner patio. ❷ Alamillos del Tránsito 13 ❶ 925 28 51 91 ❿ www.hotel-pintorelgreco.com

Abad ££ A converted 1815 blacksmith's shop in the centre of Toledo, near the most important monuments and enjoying beautiful views over the River Tagus. ❷ Real del Arrabal 1 ❶ 925 28 35 00 ❿ www.hotelabad-toledo.com

Casona de la Reyna ££ This old stone house is close to the sights of Toledo. One room has its own fireplace. Breakfast is the only meal served but there is a coffee bar. **ⓐ** Carrera de San Sebastián 26 **ⓣ** 925 28 05 52 **ⓦ** www.casonadelareyna.com

Hostal del Cardenal £££ A historic hotel next to the city walls in an 18th-century mansion, which was formerly the residence of the archbishop of Toledo. It is tastefully furnished with a mixture of old and new furniture. **ⓐ** Paseo de Recaredo 24 **ⓣ** 925 22 49 00 **ⓦ** www.hostaldelcardenal.com

Parador de Toledo £££ An out-of-town hotel that forms part of the prestigious state-run chain. It has an incomparable view of Toledo from its terrace. **ⓐ** Cerro del Emperador **ⓣ** 925 22 18 50 **ⓦ** www.paradores.es

LA MANCHA

Beyond the boundaries of Madrid province, you reach the plains of La Mancha, the stamping ground of Don Quixote and Sancho Panza. While not always scenically attractive, La Mancha does have points of interest, as well as the big advantage that it's not overrun with tourists. In the book, Don Quixote is knighted by an innkeeper who is only trying to humour him. This is supposed to have happened at the inn at Puerto Lápice, which Don Quixote imagines to be 'a fortress with its four towers and pinnacles of shining silver'. Another Quixote location is the quiet, pretty village of El Toboso. As for windmills, those that Cervantes had in mind are at Mota del Cuervo, but the best ones to see are at Consuegra and Campo de Criptana.

La Mancha has a few splashes of natural beauty too, notably the Lagunas de Ruidera and the national park of Tablas de Daimiel.

Other places worth visiting in this region are Almagro, which has a galleried main square and a Golden Age theatre, and the ruined castle-monastery of the knights of Calatrava, southeast of Ciudad Real.

⬤ One of La Mancha's famous windmills

RETAIL THERAPY

La Mancha has the largest expanse of vineyards in Spain, and a variety of wines from cheap to vintage can be bought in Valdepeñas. Manchego cheese, made from ewe's milk, is widely available and lasts perfectly well if kept cool. Ask for *curado* if you like your cheese mature and tasty, or *semicurado* if you prefer it mild.

Saffron, which is used to give paella its yellow colour, also comes from La Mancha. In autumn you'll see fields of the purple crocus from which it is harvested in brief bloom. Saffron is sold in small quantities in La Mancha's shops (and in Madrid delicatessens).

If, on the other hand, you want a non-perishable souvenir to take home from La Mancha then handmade lace is the best choice.

TAKING A BREAK

Venta del Quijote ££ A good roadside stop, this is allegedly the inn that Cervantes describes in *Don Quixote* and it is consequently geared up for camera-toting tourists. If you avoid the souvenir shop, however, this doesn't diminish its attractiveness and it surrounds a very pretty rustic courtyard. ⓐ El Molino 4, Puerto Lápice ⓣ 926 57 61 10 ⓦ www.ventadelquijote.com

ACCOMMODATION

Casa de la Torre ££ Located in El Toboso – a small village mentioned in *Don Quixote* as the home of Dulcinea, the hero's platonic lover – this hotel plays on the obvious literary theme. It is in a refurbished traditional 17th-century noble's house that has kept its original features, including a patio with a well. ⓐ Antonio Machado 16, El Toboso ⓣ 925 56 80 06 ⓦ www.casadelatorre.com

----

▶ *Madrid Metro station sign*

PRACTICAL
information

Directory

GETTING THERE

By air

Madrid's **Aeropuerto de Barajas** is served by a large number of scheduled international airlines, including several budget companies offering highly competitive fares, especially if you book online. Flying time from Britain is around 2 hours.

Iberia ☎ 902 400 500 🖐 www.iberia.com

British Airways ☎ 0844 493 0787 🖐 www.britishairways.com

easyJet ☎ 0871 244 2366 🖐 www.easyjet.com

Many people are aware that air travel emits CO_2, which contributes to climate change. You may be interested in the possibility of lessening the environmental impact of your flight through the charity **Climate Care** (🖐 www.jpmorganclimatecare.com), which offsets your CO_2 by funding environmental projects around the world.

By car

By road from Calais, head south to Biarritz and cross the frontier at the western end of the Pyrenees (between Hendaye and Irún) to reach San Sebastián. Turn inland for Vitoria-Gasteiz and pick up the NI motorway for Madrid at Burgos. Alternatively, take a ferry from Portsmouth to Bilbao or Santander and drive south to Burgos and on to Madrid.

Spain drives on the right. It is forbidden to drive under the influence of alcohol. Seat belts are obligatory and children under 12 should travel in the back. Speed limits are 120 km/h (75 mph) on motorways, 100 km/h (62 mph) on roads and 50 km/h (31 mph) in built-up areas. The police can issue on-the-spot fines for traffic offences. Most national driving licences are valid but it is advisable to have an international driving licence. Cars must have a red warning triangle, replacement light bulbs and a reflective jacket in the passenger compartment in case of emergency. Petrol (*gasolina*) comes as *normal* (leaded), *sin plomo* (unleaded) and *gasoil* (diesel).

By rail

All trains into Madrid are operated by the national company **RENFE** (📞 902 32 03 20 🌐 www.renfe.es).

To plan a rail trip from the UK to Spain, it's best to use an international agent such as **Rail Europe** (📧 34 Tower View, Kings Hill, West Malling, Kent ME19 4ED 📞 0844 848 4064 🌐 www.raileurope.co.uk). Journey time is 1½–2 days.

🔺 *Outside the new terminal at Barajas Airport*

ENTRY FORMALITIES

Visitors from the UK, Ireland, other EU countries, the USA, Canada, Australia and New Zealand require only a valid passport to enter Spain. Visitors from South Africa must have a visa. There is no restriction on what items you may bring in with you as a tourist but you'll find almost everything you need locally. In Spain you are obliged by law to carry your passport with you at all times in case the police ask for identification.

Visitors to Spain from within the EU are entitled to bring their personal effects and goods for personal consumption and not for resale. Those entering the country from outside the EU may bring 200 cigarettes (50 cigars, 250 g tobacco), 2 litres of wine or 1 litre of spirits. No meat or dairy products may be brought into the country from inside or outside the EU.

MONEY

The Spanish currency is the euro, divided into 100 centimes. There are coins of 1 and 2 euros and of 1, 2, 5, 10, 20 and 50 centimes; the notes are of 5, 10, 20, 50, 100, 200 and 500 euros.

Banks (*bancos*) are generally open only 09.00–13.30 Monday to Friday but there are many cash machines (ATMs) where you can get money out with a credit card and some debit cards. Credit cards are accepted for payment except in smaller bars and shops, and in *pensiones*. Traveller's cheques can be cashed in banks and big hotels.

HEALTH, SAFETY & CRIME

British citizens – as all EU nationals – are entitled to free treatment from the Spanish social security system on production of a European Health Insurance Card (EHIC). Many travellers prefer to take out private medical insurance for a greater choice of healthcare.

Take a few simple precautions to avoid crime: watch out for pickpockets in crowded places like the metro, markets and bars, and keep your bag across your chest and in front of you. Leave valuables in a hotel safe and never leave anything on display in a parked car. See also Emergencies (page 152).

Travel insurance, obtainable from your travel agent, airline or any insurance company, should give adequate cover not only for medical expenses but also for loss or theft of possessions, personal liability and repatriation in an emergency. If driving to Spain, ask your insurer for a green card and check on the cover you will need for damage, loss or theft of the vehicle and for legal costs in the event of an accident. If you intend to hire a car, check whether collision insurance is covered by your UK car insurance.

OPENING HOURS

Shops 09.00 or 10.00–13.30, 17.00–20.30 Mon–Sat; department stores and large shops 10.00–21.00. Many close for at least two weeks in August.

Post offices generally 09.00–14.00 Mon–Fri & 09.00–13.00 Sat.

Banks usually 09.00–13.30 Mon–Fri.

Offices 09.00–14.00, 16.00–20.00 Mon–Fri (sometimes 08.00–15.00 in summer).

Museums 09.00–13.00, 16.00–20.00 Tues–Sat and perhaps Sun morning. Usually closed Mon.

Restaurants Mealtimes in Spain are later than in the rest of Europe. Breakfast in hotels is served 07.30–10.00, lunch 14.00–16.00 and dinner 21.00–23.00. Many restaurants and bars close for at least two weeks in August.

TOILETS

Madrid has few public toilets and the most convenient thing to do is go into a bar or café – in which case it is polite to buy a drink or, at the very least, ask permission. Another option is to use those in a department store, such as El Corte Inglés (see page 66). There are several words for toilets in Spanish, the most common being *servicios*, *aseos* and *lavabos*.

CHILDREN

In Spain children simply fit into ordinary life. Although they are generally smothered with attention and greatly indulged, there is a lack of special facilities for them: for example, you are unlikely to see a 'child menu' in all but the most touristy restaurants. For younger children, there are increasing numbers of baby changing facilities, especially in large malls and department stores, but breastfeeding spaces are virtually non-existent so you'll just have to be discreet.

If you need to give the children a break from museum hopping, head to Retiro Park (see page 76), which has a boating lake, or the Casa de Campo (see page 33), which has a swimming pool. For more serious fun, there is a good choice of attractions, including Faunia, a nature theme park (see page 113), and **IMAX Madrid**, which shows films in OMNIMAX on an enormous semicircular dome, and IMAX 3D, with three-dimensional images projected on a flat screen that you watch with special glasses (ⓐ Meneses ⓣ 914 67 48 00 ⓛ 11.00–13.00, 17.00–23.00 Tues–Sun ⓜ Metro: Méndez Álvaro ⓘ Admission charge). **Snow Zone**, at Madrid's Xanadú shopping centre, has an artificial snow slope for skiing and snowboarding (ⓐ Carretera N-V Km 23.5, Arroyomolinos ⓣ 902 36 13 09 ⓦ www.madridsnowzone.com ⓛ Shopping centre 10.00–22.00; leisure facilities 10.00–24.00 Mon–Sun ⓘ Admission charge).

The **Museo del Ferrocarril (Railway Museum**, ⓐ Paseo de las Delicias 61 ⓣ 902 22 88 22 ⓦ www.museodelferrocarril.org ⓛ 10.00–15.00 Tues–Sun (closed Aug) ⓜ Metro: Delicias ⓘ Admission charge) has old steam trains and carriages, railway models and railway memorabilia. The **Parque de Atracciones** (ⓣ 902 34 50 09 ⓦ www.parquedeatracciones.es ⓛ For opening hours see website ⓜ Metro: Batán ⓘ Admission charge) is a funfair in the Casa de Campo with more than 40 rides.

The **Planetario de Madrid** (ⓐ Avenida del Planetario 16 ⓣ 914 67 34 61 ⓦ www.planetmad.es ⓛ 09.30–13.45, 17.00–19.45 Tues–Fri, 11.00–13.45, 17.00–20.45 Sat & Sun ⓜ Metro: Méndez Álvaro ⓘ Admission charge) shows various films about the solar system and galaxies. For wildlife, head just outside Madrid to **Safari Park Madrid** (ⓐ Carretera de Navalcarnero-Cadalso Km 22, Aldea del Fresno ⓣ 918 62 23 14 ⓦ www.safarimadrid.com ⓛ 10.30–19.00 ⓘ Admission charge) or the **Zoo Aquarium de Madrid** (ⓐ Casa de Campo ⓣ 902 34 50 14 ⓦ www.zoomadrid.com ⓛ 10.30–19.00 ⓜ Metro: Casa de Campo ⓘ Admission charge), which has a collection of 3,000 animals.

For **Parque Warner**, the Hollywood-oriented theme park, see page 117.

COMMUNICATION
Internet
There are still a few Internet cafés (*cafés cibernéticos*) in the city but many people prefer to use the burgeoning number of Wi-Fi hotspots in hotels and other public buildings. If you haven't got your own gear with you, one of the best places to have a coffee while checking your emails is the traditional Café Comercial (ⓐ Glorieta de Bilbao 7 ⓣ 915 21 56 55 ⓜ Metro: Bilbao.

> **TELEPHONING SPAIN**
> Spain's country code is 34. Madrid's provincial area code, 91, must be dialled before all phone numbers, even for local calls. National and international information ☎ 11888.
>
> **TELEPHONING ABROAD**
> To make an international call, dial 00 + the country code + the phone number omitting the initial zero. Country code: UK 44, USA and Canada 1, Australia 61, New Zealand 64, South Africa 27, Ireland 353.

Phone

Local, national and international calls can be made from public phone booths (*cabinas*) in the street and metro and train stations, using coins or cards. Instructions are in several languages. Some phone boxes take credit cards. Phonecards (*tarjetas telefónicas*) are on sale at tobacconists (*estancos*) and post offices.

You can also phone from *locutorios*, public telephone centres; pay at the counter when you have finished your call. Calls from a hotel room are more expensive than from phone boxes or *locutorios*.

You can find phone numbers at ⓦ www.paginasamarillas.es (the Spanish yellow pages) and ⓦ www.paginasblancas.es (the phone book). See also the website of the national phone company, Telefonica ⓦ www.telefonica.es

Post

Madrid's post offices, *correos*, are open 08.00–21.00 Monday to Friday, and 09.00–14.00 on Saturday. The main post office is the **Palacio de**

🔺 *The iconic Plaza de la Cibeles hosts the Centre of Communications for Spain*

las Comunicaciones on Plaza de la Cibeles (Ⓜ Metro: Banco de España). Postboxes are yellow with two slots, one for the city (*ciudad*) and one for other destinations. Stamps are sold in state-run tobacco shops (*estancos*); letters and postcards weighing up to 20 g cost 34 cents within Spain; 64 cents to the rest of Europe; 78 cents to the rest of the world. For further information, check the post office website Ⓦ www.correos.es. Post generally takes around five working days to arrive to the rest of Europe and eight to ten days to the USA.

ELECTRICITY

Spain's electricity supply is 220 volts. Plugs have two round pins, so UK electrical devices will need an adaptor. US (110 volts) equipment will require a current transformer in addition to an adaptor.

TRAVELLERS WITH DISABILITIES

Madrid has few facilities for travellers with disabilities but the situation is slowly changing. More information is available from **COCEMFE** (🅰 Luis Cabrera 63 ☎ 917 44 36 00 🆆 www.cocemfe.es), and the Madrid City Council publish the excellent and very thorough *Guía de Accesibilidad de Madrid* in association with the FAMMA disabled association (available through 🆆 www.famma.org).

In the UK contact **RADAR** (☎ 020 7250 3222 🆆 www.radar.org.uk) and **Holiday Care Service** (☎ 0845 124 9971 🆆 www.holidaycare.org.uk).

TOURIST INFORMATION

Before travelling, general information about Spain can be obtained from the **Spanish Tourist Office** in London. Visits are strictly by appointment (☎ 020 7486 8077 ✉ info.londres@tourspain.es 🕐 09.15–13.30 Mon–Fri). The official websites (🆆 www.tourspain.co.uk and 🆆 www.tourspain.es) will answer many basic questions.

Main tourist office in Madrid 🅰 Plaza Mayor 27 ☎ 915 88 16 36 🅼 Metro: Sol; also tourist offices in Plaza de la Cibeles, Plaza de Callao and Avenida Felipe II 🕐 09.30–20.30 daily 🆆 www.esmadrid.com

The airport and Chamartín and Atocha railway stations have information offices 🕐 08.00–20.00 Mon–Sat, 09.00–14.00 Sun

Tourist office for the provinces (including Aranjuez, El Escorial and Alcalá de Henares) 🅰 Duque de Medinaceli 2 ☎ 902 10 00 07 🆆 www.madrid.org/turismo 🕐 08.00–20.00 Mon–Sat, 09.00–14.00 Sun 🅼 Metro: Sevilla

BACKGROUND READING

Very little of note has been written specifically about Madrid in English. Hugh Thomas' *Madrid: A Traveller's Companion* is an anthology of visitors' descriptions and impressions dating from the Middle Ages to the 1930s, including Casanova and the Duke of Wellington. Michael Jacobs' *Madrid Observed* and Elizabeth Nash's *Madrid* are both personal takes on the city. As for fiction in translation, Nobel Prize winner Camilo José Cela's *The Hive* conjures up depressed post-Civil War Madrid, while Arturo Perez Reverte's *Captain Alatriste* is a swashbuckling romp through the city in the Golden Age.

For recent history, John Hooper's *The New Spaniards* is a thorough and readable account of social and political change since the death of Franco up to the 1990s. Phil Ball's *Morbo* is a history of Spanish football with good coverage on Real Madrid. Art books include Robert Hughes' *Goya* and *Velázquez: Painter and Courtier* by Jonathan Brown.

⬥ *Read all about it... a distinctive newsstand*

Emergencies

There are separate emergency numbers for the police, fire brigade
and ambulance, but the emergency number ☎ 112 will get you
through to an operator who will connect you to the service you
need. Emergency numbers are listed in telephone directories
under *Servicios de Urgencias*.

Ambulance ☎ 061/112
Fire brigade ☎ 112
Guardia Civil ☎ 062/ Madrid capital 915 14 63 24
Policía Municipal ☎ 092
Policía Nacional ☎ 091

MEDICAL SERVICES
Ambulances & hospitals
To summon an ambulance, call the general emergency number
☎ 112 or if you are left on hold for too long, try ☎ 061 ☎ 092 or call
the Cruz Roja (Spanish Red Cross) directly ☎ 902 22 22 92.

If you make straight for a hospital in a taxi, ask to be taken to
Hospital La Paz (☎ Paseo de la Castellana 261, Chamartín ☎ 917 27 70 00
Ⓜ Metro: Begoña). Accident and Emergency is called *Urgencias*. For
English-speaking help, contact:
British American Medical Unit ☎ Conde de Aranda 1 ☎ 914 35 18 23
Ⓜ Metro: Retiro
Clinica Dental ☎ Calle Magallanes 18 ☎ 914 46 32 21 Ⓜ Metro: Quevedo
Ⓦ www.clinicadentalcisne.com

Pharmacies
Minor health problems can often be cleared up by consulting a *farmacia*
(pharmacy), which is indicated by a lighted green cross sign. Pharmacists

are trained to advise on common ailments. Out of hours, there is always a *farmacia de guardia* open in every neighbourhood; you'll find its address posted in the window of other *farmacias*.

POLICE

Madrid effectively has three police forces. The Policía Municipal is responsible for traffic problems and low level policing; the Policía Nacional is in charge of more serious crime and the paramilitary Guardia Civil takes care of highway patrols and customs. You can turn to any of them in the event of an emergency.

There are police stations at Atocha and Chamartín railway stations and in the Puerta del Sol but your best bet is the **Comisaría del Centro** (📍 Calle Leganitos 19 🚇 Metro: Plaza de España or Santo Domingo), which has a service for tourists with interpreters. You can contact the police for information or to make a complaint on 📞 902 10 21 12 or see 🌐 www.policia.es

🔺 *Mounted police patrol the streets and parks of Madrid*

EMBASSIES & CONSULATES

Australia 🅐 Torre Espacio, Paseo de la Castellana 259D
🅣 913 53 66 00 🅦 www.embaustralia.es 🅝 Metro: Begoña
Canada 🅐 Nuñez de Balboa 35 🅣 914 23 32 50 🅝 Metro: Velázquez
Ireland 🅐 Paseo de la Castellana 46 🅣 914 36 40 93
🅝 Metro: Rubén Darío
New Zealand 🅐 Calle Pinar 7, 3rd floor 🅣 915 23 02 26
🅦 www.nzembassy.com 🅝 Metro: Gregorio Marañón
South Africa 🅐 Claudio Coello 91 🅣 914 36 37 80 🅝 Metro: Rubén Darío
UK 🅐 Torre Espacio, Paseo de la Castellana 259D 🅣 917 14 64 00
🅦 www.ukinspain.com 🅝 Begoña
USA 🅐 Calle Serrano 75 🅣 915 87 22 00 🅦 www.embusa.es
🅝 Metro: Rubén Darío

EMERGENCY PHRASES

Help!	**Fire!**	**Stop!**
¡Socorro!	¡Fuego!	¡Stop!
¡Sawkoro!	¡Fwegoh!	¡Stop!

Call an ambulance/a doctor/the police/the fire service!
¡Llame a una ambulancia/un médico/la policía/a los bomberos!
¡Lliame a oona anboolanthea/oon meydico/la poletheea/
a lohs bombehrohs!

⬤ *Atocha Station has a veritable oasis at its centre*

ACKNOWLEDGEMENTS

The publishers would like to thank the following individuals and organisations for supplying their copyright photographs for this book: BigStockPhoto.com pages 31 (Gary718), 143 (Jonathan Borzicchi); Camper page 97; Dreamstime.com pages 5 & 77 (Tupungato), 29 (Robert Paul van Beets), 119 (Rainer Walter Schmeid), 141 (Andrew Chambers); Imagebrokers/Photoshot page 93); iStockphoto.com pages 32 (João Saraiva), 101 (Kevin George), 153 (Manuel Velasco); Pictures Colour Library pages 17, 21 (Paul Gibson), 83; Luciá Pizarro Coma/SXC.hu page 155; Rusticae/Hotel Room Mate Mario page 39; Turespaña pages 40–41, 45, 55, 110–11; Turespaña/Plaza de la Cibeles Madrid page 149; Wikimedia Commons pages 47 & 71; Nick Inman all others.

Project editor: Tom Lee
Proofreaders: Jan McCann & Caroline Hunt
Layout: Donna Pedley

Send your thoughts to
books@thomascook.com

- Found a great bar, club, shop or must-see sight that we don't feature?

- Like to tip us off about any information that needs a little updating?

- Want to tell us what you love about this handy little guidebook and more importantly how we can make it even handier?

Then here's your chance to tell all! Send us ideas, discoveries and recommendations today and then look out for your valuable input in the next edition of this title.

Email the above address (stating the title) or write to:
pocket guides Series Editor, Thomas Cook Publishing, PO Box 227, Coningsby Road, Peterborough PE3 8SB, UK.

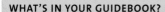

WHAT'S IN YOUR GUIDEBOOK?

Independent authors Impartial up-to-date information from our travel experts who meticulously source local knowledge.

Experience Thomas Cook's 165 years in the travel industry and guidebook publishing enriches every word with expertise you can trust.

Travel know-how Thomas Cook has thousands of staff working around the globe, all living and breathing travel.

Editors Travel-publishing professionals, pulling everything together to craft a perfect blend of words, pictures, maps and design.

You, the traveller We deliver a practical, no-nonsense approach to information, geared to how you really use it.

Useful phrases

English	Spanish	Approx pronunciation
BASICS		
Yes	Sí	Si
No	No	Noh
Please	Por favor	Por fabor
Thank you	Gracias	Grathias
Hello	Hola	Ola
Goodbye	Adiós	Adios
Excuse me	Disculpe	Diskoolpeh
Sorry	Perdón	Pairdohn
That's okay	De acuerdo	Dey acwerdo
I don't speak Spanish	No hablo español	Noh ablo espanyol
Do you speak English?	¿Habla Usted inglés?	¿Abla oosteth eengless?
Good morning	Buenos días	Bwenos dee-as
Good afternoon	Buenas tardes	Bwenas tarrdess
Good evening	Buenas noches	Bwenas notchess
Goodnight	Buenas noches	Bwenas notchess
My name is ...	Me llamo ...	Meh yiamo ...
NUMBERS		
One	Uno	Oono
Two	Dos	Dos
Three	Tres	Tres
Four	Cuatro	Cwatro
Five	Cinco	Thinco
Six	Seis	Seys
Seven	Siete	Seeyetey
Eight	Ocho	Ocho
Nine	Nueve	Nwebeyh
Ten	Diez	Deeyeth
Twenty	Veinte	Beintey
Fifty	Cincuenta	Thincwenta
One hundred	Cien	Thien
SIGNS & NOTICES		
Airport	Aeropuerto	Aehropwerto
Rail station	Estación de trenes	Estathion de trenes
Platform	Vía	Vía
Smoking/	Fumadores/	Foomadoores/
non-smoking	No fumadores	No foomadores
Toilets	Servicios	Serbitheeos
Ladies/Gentlemen	Señoras/Caballeros	Senyoras/Kabayeros